LEANING ON GOD

LEANING ON GOD

SERMONS OF RABBI CAROLE L. MEYERS

EDITED BY THE HONORABLE RALPH ZAREFSKY
FOREWORD BY RABBI DAVID ELLENSON

Copyright © 2018 by Ralph Zarefsky

Published By Steel Cut Press
www.steelcutpress.com

All rights reserved. This book, or parts thereof, may not be reproduced in any form without permission from the publisher.

Library of Congress Cataloguing Number (LCCN) - 2018940459

ISBN Paperback: 978-1-936380-11-4
ISBN Ebook Kindle: 978-1-936380-13-8
ISBN ePub: 978-1-936380-12-1

Cover painting by Oren Giladi. Used with permission of the artist.

Book design by Creative Publishing Book Design
www.creativepublishingdesign.com

In Memory of

Irving Meyers
(1918-1971)

Hortense Singer Meyers Daitz Zwick
(1920-2003)

In Honor of

Joe Zarefsky
(1993 -   )

Gus Zarefsky
(1997 -   )

TABLE OF CONTENTS

Acknowledgments   XI
Introduction   XIII
Foreword   XVII

PROLOGUE

I Hate Writing Sermons   3

I | LOSS, EVIL, FAITH

Leaning on God, Part I: Life or Death?   11
There is Meaning to be Wrested From Death   20
A Letter to God About Death   29
Suicide   36
Reacting to Evil: The Lesson of Job   43
The World is Very Dangerous   48
Evil and Faith   57
Faith in the Unknown   65

II | THE WORLD AROUND US

Marking Kristallnacht   71
News From the Outside World (March 1994)   78
A Journey Through France (1991)   83
Precious Legacy   89
Just and Unjust Wars   96

III | OUR EMOTIONAL LIVES

Anger	103
Reconciliation	110
Hope	115
Personal Prayer	120
Doubt	124
Joy and Sorrow	132
Trust	141

IV | CHANGE AND RITUAL

Leaning on God, Part II: Saying Goodbye (1986)	151
Saying Hello (1986)	158
An Early Woman Scholar	164
An Early Woman Leader	168
Homelessness	175
Wrestling With Ritual	179
A Rabbinic Community Changes (1989)	186
Homosexuality and Judaism (1990)	193
Interfaith Weddings (1997)	202
Language and the Past	212

V | GOD

God Language	225
What It Means to be Chosen	232
Our Part of the Covenant	237
Blessing: A Connection to God	242
God's Four Blessings to Us	246
Holiness	251
Small Steps	256

Letting Go	260
The Power to Move Forward	267

EPILOGUE

Leaning on God, Part III: Eulogy on the Death of Rabbi Carole Meyers	275

ACKNOWLEDGMENTS

The Quiet Faith of Man
Words and Music by Bill Staines
Copyright © 1988 Mineral River Music
All Rights Administered by BMG Rights Management (US) LLC
All Rights Reserved. Used by Permission.
Reprinted by Permission of Hal Leonard LLC

Comment, The New Yorker, May 7, 1984
Authored by William McKibben
Used With Permission from the Author

INTRODUCTION

I married Carole Meyers in December 1990. When I buried her sixteen and a half years later, I was left with sadness, grief, two minor children, and four banker's boxes of sermons. Time worked its wonder with the first three. The last was left to me.

I began with foolscap. Carole was just advancing into the technological age when she died, and she had written almost all her sermons by hand, on lined yellow legal paper. These all required review and then transcription, and, after culling out a selection of them, I turned to a talented group to input them into the computer. I deeply thank Janet Cassidy, Kay Fransson, Margie Martinez, Valencia Munroe and Nikki Zarefsky for diligently and selflessly converting scribble into print.

A sermon is a unique form of communication, combining many disciplines and forms. It begins with theology, of course, but easily moves into ethics, psychology, human and community relations, and practical living. It can be a conversation or an oration, prodding, cajoling, instructing or criticizing – or all of these. Its power derives both from its substance and from its presentation.

Rabbi Carole Meyers was a gifted speaker. She had a gentle, lyrical voice, an animated face, a wide and warm smile, and a fluid speaking style. Rarely was she harsh; frequently she mixed analytical thought with vivid imagery; sometimes she interwove music into the sermon; always she sought meaning from Biblical text. Those who heard her speak from the pulpit came away enriched, feeling an emotional connection and often the awakening of a dormant spiritual life. I believe that those who heard some or all of these sermons will be able, upon re-reading them, to close their eyes, hear her voice, and see the twinkle in her eyes as she says again and again, "Now, really, *this* is my favorite Torah portion."

This collection of Rabbi Meyers' sermons, however, speaks to both those who heard them and to new readers as well. As my long-time friend and mentor, Reverend David A. Jones, Professor Emeritus of History at North Carolina Wesleyan College has said, the task of a re-printed sermon is "to evoke the sermon for those who were there, and imagine it for those who were not." Those who were not there to hear Carole Meyers preach cannot know the full power of the experience, but – just as we can appreciate Lincoln's words or know the impact of Jonathan Edwards' jeremiads without having heard them – the sermons presented here carry force for their ideas, their phrasing and their themes.

One major theme explored in these sermons is the concept of loss. Carole's father died when she was 13; her mother re-married, and the new step-father died when Carole was 19. These early experiences with death shaped the rabbi Carole would become, and throughout

Introduction

her life Carole looked for meaning in the experience of death and loss. Always she would ask what she could learn from these experiences, what lessons the universe was trying to teach her. Always she would bring to bear on those questions her learning in theology, her study of philosophy and her empathy for people.

A closely-related theme, and one Carole often explored, was the nature of God. Her interest in becoming a rabbi also began with her father's death, when the local rabbi comforted her and she began to see the power of the rabbinate to help explain the world. At that time, of course, there were no women rabbis, but nevertheless she had hold of an early concept of Godliness that began to drive her. She continued to evolve her thoughts, and one can see, in these sermons, a view of God that is sometimes questioning, critical or frustrated, but ultimately embracing: God is a force to lean on.

The ideas here are not unique, but they are powerfully expressed, and of course have benefited over the years from the insights of others. Carole learned at the feet of master teachers Eugene Borowitz, Norman Cohen and Lawrence Hoffman at the Hebrew Union College in New York. After ordination, she grew immensely under the wise guidance of Rabbi Samuel Karff of Congregation Beth Israel in Houston. After she assumed her own pulpit at Temple Sinai of Glendale in California, she regularly met with colleagues from other parts of the country, Rabbis Stacy Offner, Judy Shanks, Margaret Moers Wenig and Marjorie Yudkin, to share sermon ideas and discuss theological and practical issues. All of these people will find parts of their own ideas expressed in these sermons.

I turned to some of these same people when I had assembled these sermons, and asked them to review them for me. I thank these good friends and others – now my friends as well as formerly

Carole's – for their thoughts and help: Rabbis Offner, Wenig, Susan Einbinder and William Cutter, and our good friend Mary Baron, all of whom read some or all of the sermons and offered their thoughts, and Provost Emeritus Norman Cohen, who assisted with the publication of the volume.

I have dedicated this book to Rabbi Meyers' inheritance – her parents, Irving Meyers and Hortense Singer Meyers Daitz Zwick – and to Rabbi Meyers' legacy – our sons Joe and Gus Zarefsky. May the former rest in peace, and the latter continue to heal the world.

Ralph Zarefsky
La Cañada-Flintridge, California
September 2017

FOREWORD

When I was a rabbinical student at Hebrew Union College-Jewish Institute of Religion during the 1970s, our Professor of Homiletics Rabbi Leonard Kravitz told us that as preachers the foremost rule we had to follow was that we should always be ourselves. Our words had to flow not only from our minds, but had to express the very depths of our being and the sincerity of our souls. As he taught us, "Words that come from the heart, enter into the hearts of another." Rabbi Kravitz said that we also had to be mindful of a second cardinal principle when we spoke from the pulpit. He expressed this principle by citing the familiar Hebrew words, "*Va'ydaber Moshe el b'nei yisrael, va-yee'sa-oo,*" which he translated as, "When Moses our Rabbi spoke to the Children of Israel, they were moved." It was not enough to instruct. The preacher was required to move the congregation and those who sat in it.

Leaning on God

As I read these sermons of Rabbi Carole Meyers, I thought of what Rabbi Kravitz transmitted so long ago. In her sermons, the depth and extraordinary caring of her being and the wisdom and beauty of her mind and soul leap off the page, and they possess the remarkable power to move the reader now as they surely did when she spoke with her congregation throughout her career. She surely followed in the tradition of Moses our Rabbi as Rabbi Kravitz outlined it, and was a worthy bearer of the rabbinic title.

The sermons bespeak Carole herself. She was a gentle and thoughtful person. Kindness and calm marked her persona. At the same time, Carole possessed great knowledge and firm convictions. Her love of Judaism was palpable, as was her love of the Jewish people and the State of Israel. Carole loved people, her congregants and most of all her family. All these commitments and characteristics are evident in every word she spoke in this volume.

Carole Meyers frequently spoke in her sermons as a "prophet," always offering her community clear moral guidance on the issues of the day. She did not hesitate to address contemporaneous matters of pressing import, and she prodded her flock to be ever better persons. However, her modest soul never allowed her to pontificate. The power of her sermons is displayed in a layered and sensitive mind that never oversimplified.

In all her sermons, Carole also shared. She had a generosity of soul, and did not hesitate to use the sermon in her role as a pastor. Carole comforted her congregants when they were in distress through the compassion and empathy of her words. Their pain was hers and she cared for the members of her community as a shepherd watches over her sheep.

Foreword

As one reads these sermons, it is also equally true that her great faith in God is revealed. Hers was a mature vision of the Divine, and on every page you feel an element of privacy, a personal conversation between Carole and God as mediated through the sources of Jewish tradition. It was and remains a privilege to hear these conversations and witness the faith they express.

The midrash, in its commentary on *The Song of Songs*, states that "one who teaches Torah should make their words and deeds as sweet and as pleasant as honey from the honeycomb." Rabbi Carole Meyers was the embodiment of these words throughout her career, and her sermons testify to the character and wisdom of this remarkable teacher of Torah.

When we educate students for the rabbinate at the Hebrew Union College, we hope that each will become a *marbitzah Torah*, a teacher of Torah who lovingly and judiciously instructs and guides her congregation and her congregants with the teachings and values of our tradition. At the same time we hope that each will be a *haverah*, a friend who is always present in times of distress and pain, as well as joy and celebration. And as a *hachamah*, a wise and insightful counselor, we desire that each will provide appropriate guidance and counsel that springs from the depths of heart and soul, knowledge and mind. Happy are we that Carole Meyers was in our midst, that we had the gift of her life, and that we now possess the ongoing gift of her voice and her words.

Shir HaShirim (Song of Songs) 7:10, reads, "Moving gently the lips of those that are asleep." In their midrashic commentary upon these words, our Ancient Sages taught that this meant, "*Sif-to'tav do-ve'vot min ha-kever* – their lips move from the grave." In *Leaning on God*, the lips of Rabbi Carole Meyers move from their place of eternal rest to provide us with her continuing inspiration and singular guidance. For the gift of this book and the blessings that overflow in its pages, we have reason to be grateful.

>Rabbi David Ellenson, Chancellor Emeritus
>Hebrew Union College-Jewish Institute of Religion
>September 2017
>Waltham, Massachusetts

PROLOGUE

Prologue

I HATE WRITING SERMONS*

I approach this lectern with a sheaf of yellow papers in my hand, just as I do almost every Friday night in my congregation. In these pages are words that I have pulled from somewhere deep inside myself, words that I pray will represent some thought or insight I have had, well enough to inspire or teach those who listen. It can be a very long walk, those few steps from the rabbi's chair to the lectern. Each step calls to mind some agonized moment from the process of creating the sermon, and my anxiety blossoms. Is the idea in the sermon really something worth talking about? Are the images interesting and expressive? Does the whole piece hang together in a way that is going to communicate well?

---

*Delivered while Alumna in Residence at Hebrew Union College, New York, New York, on November 15, 1990.

I hate writing sermons. It is the hardest thing I do in my rabbinate, week in and week out. It is also one of the absolutely most important. Preaching is an activity worthy of a large investment of time and attention, and it has the potential to bring me, as a rabbi, great satisfaction and joy. Oftentimes, my first step in writing a sermon is to take a nap.

When I got up from my nap preceding this sermon, I went to the text and read "Rebekah was barren" – of ideas, I thought. And I felt her pain in my own sense of barrenness and emptiness and dryness. Later, Rebekah cries out: *Im ken, lama ze anochi*? If it is to be this way, why is this my existence? Why have I chosen to be a rabbi and to inflict this burden on myself week after week? Do I really want to go through all this the rest of my life?

I imagine that there are those blessed few of you out there who do not suffer in this way with preaching, that ideas come easily to you and words flow smoothly – but know that you are not alone if that blank page stares back at you for a long time, or if it is a profound act of faith for you to believe that the sermon will get written.

Why is it so hard to write a sermon? First, there are the voices shouting an endless din of questions in the mind: What's important enough to talk about? What's anything to talk about? Where are these people in their lives? Where am I? What matters right now to me, to them? Even beginning to answer such questions requires intense focus and concentration. It involves the task of becoming as tuned in to life, to existence, to the self, to the congregation, to happenings, as you can be. It is intense, and it is exhausting.

Second, we tend to come to the task with extraordinarily high expectations. You picture yourself, standing up there looking out at all the expectant faces and say to yourself: Argh! How can I satisfy them? You feel compelled to give them a complete justification of Judaism: say why it is important, describe all its richness, teach why it matters, why and how each of them should be active, committed Jews. Along the way, you want to convince them that life is good, that evil can be coped with, that we are all capable of leading moral, dignified lives.

No wonder it is hard.

And in and around all this, another feeling begins to demand attention. Somewhere in you, you start to wonder: Why should they pay any attention to what I have to say anyway? Who am I to stand up in front of people and tell them what I think, maybe even what to do? Why should they listen to me? The ego of it all begins to make itself felt.

The voices can be silenced, with enough work, and the expectations can be lowered to a reasonable level. But this question of where we get our authority to speak to people in this very unusual way calls out to be considered. Surely, our authority comes from the text. We are taught to read, to study, to consult commentaries, to consider and quote the interpretations of others. My first-round pattern is still to open books, looking for insights and opinions and points of view.

But there is another level to this issue of which we rarely speak. As much as we are responsible to study text and teach it, by virtue of being called "Rabbi" we are also called upon to share *ourselves*. The task that is incumbent upon each one of us is to share just that with our congregants, the deepest parts of *ourselves*, our personal understandings and insights. Thus, Isaac says to his son: "May I give you my innermost blessing before I die."

As much as our authority derives from the text, so too it derives from our innermost being. The authentic, real, deepest parts of ourselves that speak to us about God, about the afterlife, about the needs of human beings, about anything, about everything that matters – that real, clear, intensely-felt inner message, our own interpretation, is as critical to our preaching, to our authority as rabbis, as anything else.

It is not a strong ego you need to stand before a congregation to preach; you need to have something you *believe*, in the deepest parts of you. Not only does Isaac wish to *give* his innermost blessing, but it is what Jacob *asks* for, in the very same words: "Give me your innermost blessing."

Our congregants need to know from us at our innermost. They need to know that we are not only representing a tradition from the past, but that in the process of interacting with that tradition and bringing it to them, something has resonated in our own souls. Our right to preach, our authority, comes as much from undergoing this process, as it comes from studying texts. We dare not diminish the extent to which our authority comes from our innermost being.

This conviction leads to yet another difficulty in writing sermons and suggests a response to it. It is so easy to become caught up in worrying about the listeners' evaluation of the sermon. Will they agree with what I am saying? Will it anger or shock them, soothe them or comfort them? Will they like it . . . will they like *me*? Of course, we care how people will react to our sermons and we write with an eye towards their needs. But we cannot write with an eye towards their judgment of us.

If I start focusing on how each of you will respond to my sermon, whether you will agree or disagree with me, I have failed. I must focus on what I can say to you that's true, and real for me. I turn again to Isaac who said of Rebekah: "She is my sister," not "She is my wife."

Afraid of consequences, second-guessing Avimelech's reaction, he was unable to speak the truth. That it was not the truth surfaced so quickly. We cannot be afraid to say "my wife." We cannot be afraid to say the truth, as we experience it, in our sermons.

When we can speak in this way, when we can draw on our knowledge of traditional texts and teach them, while combining them with our own solid internal understanding, preaching can be pure joy. It can touch people, move them, help them open their minds and hearts. Preaching can move from being a burden we have to endure every week to being a privilege entrusted to us. If we are willing to devote the time and effort to go through this process each week, we can move from being rabbis who avoid preaching, to being rabbis who zealously protect our precious sermon time.

Still, giving sermons is risky business. It is anxiety-provoking and it is hard. What do you do when you're staring at that blank piece of paper?

My colleague Rabbi Robert Kahn, in Houston, Texas, taught me: you pray. What does he pray? "May the words of my mouth and the meditations of my heart be acceptable to you . . . ."

In the end, I am able to write when I write not only to my congregants, but to God, and for God, when I write an offering to God, and I pray from the depths of my soul: may these words that I am going to pull out from my innermost being and write on this sheaf of yellow paper be acceptable to *You*, O God, be a worthy offering to the one who is my Rock, to the only one who can redeem me.

I
LOSS, EVIL, FAITH

LEANING ON GOD, PART I: LIFE OR DEATH?

He came to me, an older man, preparing for major surgery. He was so scared and vulnerable. He said: "How do I prepare? What do I do? Give me some guidance for this moment." I said: "Syd, now is the time to count on your relationship with God. Lean on it. Pray. Let God's presence support you through this, and believe that everything will be all right."

He said: "I don't have a relationship with God. I don't even know what you mean by relationship with God."

I was stunned. This was a good Jew, a man involved in Jewish life, who supports Jewish institutions. He's attended services on and off for probably fifty years; he's raised Jewish kids. This is a man who is competent enough to lead a service or give a *d'var Torah*.

All the same, he is a man who, when forced to come face to face with his own mortality, could not say: "Be with me, God. I need your strength."

More and more, I see that he is not alone. We come. We read the prayer book. We sing. We develop relationships with like-minded people. We make sure our kids get a Jewish education, and we identify as part of the Jewish people.

But, when that moment comes, when we are sitting stone-faced in the intensive care waiting room, or are lying on a gurney, waiting to be rolled into surgery, or are in the hospital room, holding the hand of someone we love, watching them die, it is the rare one of us who can count on a relationship with God. Instead, most of us feel alone, abandoned, full of questions about who God is and where God is, and angry about how God could let such a thing happen.

There are these moments in our lives, when we need to be able to have a conversation with God. But we don't know how. I was taught in rabbinic school that you can't talk theology with people who are in this state, and my own experience has borne that out. I can't reach through the layers of exhaustion, anger, and fear that keep people from hearing how God's presence might be real for them. All I can do at such a moment is give support and warmth, hold on tight, and will someone strength.

But, I've also learned that when the moment passes, most people lose interest, they lose the motivation to put in the energy and work required to face these questions, to forge a relationship with God.

I come before you on this *Yom Kippur* evening to say: Now is the time for us to do it. Now is the time, when we make ourselves believe we are standing on the threshold of death, when the goal is for us to come to the end of *N'eilah*, the closing service, feeling as if we have

Life or Death?

stepped back from the precipice, ashen-faced, having come so close to death, and yet survived. Now is the time to ask how we can develop a relationship with God that comes with us to that place, so that when we face it in the real world, we are not so vulnerable, so pitifully alone.

What are the obstacles to having a conversation with God?

Syd said to me: "What can you possibly mean by conversation? You're surely not suggesting that there's some kind of God in the world that actually talks back to you."

No, not in words, anyway. And that raises the most basic problem we need to confront: somehow finding a way to root out this idea of God as a being, like you and me, talking, walking, thinking, only better, bigger: a superhuman – us, were we all-powerful and all-knowing. This is the God who talks to people, who tells them what to do, who rewards good acts and punishes bad ones. This is the God we hear being preached at us, by TV evangelists or by more traditional religious types. It's probably the idea of God we were taught about as children in Religious School.

I ask you: Is there any other idea we learned as children that we have not become more sophisticated about, as we have matured? Would we say that mathematics is about learning the multiplication tables, or that English is about spelling tests?

Yet, we are stuck with this childish understanding of God, because adults have been too shy, too scared, to attempt to describe their understanding of God, and they most certainly have not been willing to explain these feelings and understandings to children. So most of us grew up thinking that the only God we could believe in was a God who could do anything, who could answer all your prayers, who could talk to you in words. And if we didn't have an experience of that God, we concluded, we didn't believe in God.

Yes, I believe it is possible to have a conversation with God. It is possible to let the words spill out of you, in a free, uncensored way, the fears, the anxiety, the pain, the pleas; and it is possible to sense a response, to feel that you have been heard, and to feel a strength welling up within. It is possible to find a conduit to the very best parts of yourself, to the part that is wise, courageous and good. It is possible to feel that at the most terrible times of aloneness and of vulnerability, you are not alone – that there is a Presence, a comforting Presence, listening, watching, supporting.

It is time to be sophisticated enough about our theology to let ourselves think of all these terms, listening, watching, supporting, even of God, Godself, as metaphor.

Do I believe that God has ears with which to hear? Or eyes with which to see? I do not. But these words are the best our limited human way of communicating, with language, allow us. And these images worked, as long as they were understood to be metaphor. But somewhere along the way, we lost track of the fact that all of these expressions were just that, expressions, metaphors, pointing to a reality far beyond anything we could describe in words.

But I tell you, there is a Presence that can make itself known to you, and can help.

Syd said: "You pray and you pray and the bad thing happens anyway. You can pray for your father all day in that waiting room and he could die anyway."

That's right. People pray for things all the time that they don't get.

Two comments. One, who do we think we are, that we know whether someone should live or die? All we know is what we want, what we think would make our lives better. The God I trust in would have a somewhat wider perspective than this. There is so much going

Life or Death?

on in creation that we cannot begin to understand. Why do we think we know whether someone should live or die, that we know what is meaningful in the grand scheme of things? Most of us only have about a fifty-fifty shot at making a correct decision in our own lives. What makes us think we know what should happen to create a more meaningful, a more just world?

Which leads to the second comment: Perhaps we are praying for the wrong things. To ask that a life be spared or that a surgery go well is so human and so understandable, but if the answer to that prayer is no, that the person is meant to die, that the surgery must fail, then, perhaps, we must accept that answer to the prayer, the prayer was answered, and perhaps with more wisdom than we could possibly comprehend. And then, we need to turn to a different kind of prayer, the prayers that ask for understanding, for strength, for the courage to persevere.

Syd said: "What if God is just something human beings made up to make themselves feel better?"

What if that's true? So what? If the idea of God can help us create Godliness in our world, that's enough for me. Prayer to such a God is still meaningful. It still helps us find strength beyond our own strength, a calm that can lead to acceptance. This is prayer, then, that draws us to the deepest and finest parts of ourselves, parts of us it is sometime nearly impossible to find.

And what if God *isn't* something human beings made up to make themselves feel better? Then we have the possibility of being part of something so much beyond what we are, that it can surely help us find understanding, strength, and courage that we could not find on our own. Then – now, remember, this is a metaphor – then we can be as if lifted on eagle's wings, upheld, and carried, swiftly, and surely.

Personally? My own experience? I'll tell you. I believe I have had the experience of being enveloped, momentarily, in a Godly presence. I believe there was something, outside of myself, that was there, and knew, and heard. I felt it. Not in the normal way, not with weight, or pressure against me, but in some way, it was there.

Syd said: "I don't believe in God."

Most people don't at the start. Belief doesn't come in a flash; it's not something you have or don't have. It has to grow. If I could prove it to you, in a concrete way, then you would believe it. Big deal. That's why we call it belief, because it requires tentative steps, ever-deepening experiences, until you come to an understanding, a sensing of something that has not been made plain to human beings, but may, nevertheless, exist. For most of us, there's not a moment when you suddenly believe. Instead, it's a process, during which, at some point, you begin to have a different feeling about God.

"How?" he said. "How would I start, if I wanted to start?" He was scared enough, at that moment, to be motivated to try.

Prayer, I think. I think that prayer is the way in. The goal is to get to a place where you feel comfortable enough to pray spontaneously, where your relationship to God is a given, and you can silently, almost as a form of meditation, open your heart up fully and completely, to that God.

To get there, first try some more formal prayer. One written set of prayers I suggest are the morning blessings, a series of one-line blessings, acknowledging the possibility of God's presence in everyday acts. They are blessings to actually be said in the morning, as you complete specific actions, like waking up, sitting up in bed, placing your feet on the ground. Each one is intended to remind you that each of these actions is a small miracle in itself. Each suggests that God's presence is somehow behind it all.

Life or Death?

A second possibility is to revive the traditional practice of saying the *Shema* just before you go to sleep. You can leave it at that, or you can use this moment, between wakefulness and sleep, to go a bit deeper, to consider the events of the day, to offer them up to God, to be open to help with them, or to a sense of their being blessed. Start slowly. Don't expect much. But if you stick with it, you may begin to pray.

A third possible moment is when you enter and exit your house. Why? Let the *mezuzah* call out to you. You don't have to stop and kiss it in the traditional way . . . or you can. But notice it. Every now and then, pause for a moment, physically, if you can, mentally if not, and imagine the Divine Presence, let it speak to you. Let it help you notice who you are, what you are doing, what your place is in this universe. Let it lead you into a moment of prayer.

A fourth possibility is visiting cemeteries. This is a trickier one for me to talk about, because I'm not sure exactly what makes prayer more likely in a cemetery. I only know they are holy places, filled with untold amounts of human experience. They are places where, perhaps more than any other, human beings and God reach out for each other, trying to make a connection, trying to brush souls. When you visit the grave of someone you love, take a moment to pray. Not exactly talking to that person, but using that sacred space to begin another conversation. Or just go. You don't have to be visiting a particular grave. Just be there, with all the prayers of those who came there before you, the spoken and the unspoken prayers, be there with all the yearning of human beings towards God, and see if you can feel God's yearning in return.

Syd said: "It sounds crazy. Or if not crazy, then for someone really religious, for someone, well, wackier, than I am."

I know. I know it sounds crazy. Or, it sounds spiritual, in the slightly insulting usage of that term. But I also know you have to begin somewhere, if you hope to be able to pray to God before the surgery.

So you have to start having the conversation with God in your normal, daily life, because you can't start in a crisis. It will be awkward at first. Think about the closest relationships you have in your life. Remember back to when you first met those people. There was probably shy, awkward conversation. Small talk. A question in the back of your mind about whether this was a person you might be able to become close to. Remember those first, casual conversations, and the weeks, or months, or years over which you became closer, learning more about each other, about how to talk to each other, what to expect from each other, until one day you noticed that they really understood you, and you them. You discovered that there was trust between you. You couldn't have known from the start the richness, the joy that would eventually exist between you.

A relationship with God has to be forged. And it has to be tended to, like any other relationship. It doesn't just happen.

Is it possible on this *Yom Kippur* to motivate you to try, so that when I meet you in the intensive care waiting room, or lying in that hospital bed, you will know what I'm talking about when I say: "Lean on your relationship with God. Let it support you now."

Because I do believe, with all my soul, that when you are at your most vulnerable, in the places where no friend, no lover, can follow you, you do not have to be utterly alone. There exists a Presence that can be with you, to ease your way and calm your spirit.

On Shabbat, we often pray these words: "We dare not wait for peace to fall like rain upon us. We must do the work of peace

Life or Death?

ourselves." On this day when we Jews imagine that we are at death's door, and we are presenting ourselves before God, I say we dare not wait for a closeness with God to fall like rain upon us. We must do the work of forging that relationship ourselves, or it will be lost to us.

And we need it. We need it so badly.

So this *Kol Nidre*, I pray: O God, be with us, when we reach out to you. Make yourself known to us. In the words of the Psalms: "Do not go so far away, leaving us abandoned and alone, but hold us close. Hold us in your right hand."

Baruch atah Adonai. Blessed is the Holy One;

Eloheynu melech ha-olam. The God who can be present to us;

Shomea tefillah. The One who has the capacity to hear our prayer.

And let us say: Amen.

THERE IS MEANING TO BE WRESTED FROM DEATH

And so we come to find ourselves gathered together in our sanctuary at the holiest hour of our communal life. *Yom Kippur* evening, the most mysterious, sacred, haunting time. Our sacred space is filled tonight with our bodies and our souls; with souls that were and those that are yet to be. It is filled with all our longings, passions, and goals, with our guilts, our triumphs, and sorrows, and our losses.

Most particularly this year, the sanctuary is filled with our losses. Each week, we have among us those who are observing *shloshim*. Each week, we read the list of names of the people our community is mourning. The list gets longer and longer.

It has been a hard year of loss for our community. We have buried members of our congregation, and spouses of our members. We have mourned for the child of a member and tried to console

There is Meaning to be Wrested from Death

a bereaved mother. We have mourned for friends and for strangers. The newspapers are filled with unspeakable acts of violence and we have taken the victims and their families into our hearts with our own. And we have mourned so many parents. We move from house to house, gathering for the *shiva minyans*, our voices rising in prayer to support those staggering beneath the weight of the realization of a parent gone.

Perhaps it is because our congregation is growing larger. Perhaps because so many of our members are at the time of life when their parents are aging rapidly. Sometimes it seems as if the cancers are more present and more vicious than ever before, and sometimes it seems that this community has just had more than its share of grieving and loss.

For whatever reason, this year has seen us both weeping for those we have lost and standing strong as pillars in support of those who mourn.

This liturgy of this *Yom Kippur* reverberates in our hearts: On *Rosh Hashanah* it is written; on *Yom Kippur* it is sealed. How many shall pass on, how many shall come to be. Who shall live and who shall die.

But this year, what we have been reminded of so dramatically is that all of us who live, will die. The fact of our own mortality, and the mortality of those we hold dear, comes and goes in our minds and hearts. We hold on to the idea briefly – one day my father will die; someday, my spouse will die. What will it be like when I am the one who is dying? We let our minds roam for a moment, imagining how we will cope, what we will do, and then we pull back sharply. No, we say, we won't think about that, we don't need to think about that . . . and mostly, we don't. But this *Yom Kippur* of the year of our loss, this day when we pull back the curtains, and strive to see things as they truly are, perhaps there are a few things to be said about the struggle all of us have facing death in our lives.

Listen to what we learn from our ancestors. Sarah is the first of them to die, at the age of 127 years, in Hebron, after the near-death of her son Isaac. Abraham follows, at 175; he breathed his last at a good, ripe age, old and contented, and was gathered to his kin. Isaac marries Rebecca just after his mother's death, and finds comfort. When he was 60, his sons were born, and, with thirteen grandchildren, he dies in Hebron at 180 years old. The Torah says: "He was gathered to his kin in ripe, old age, and buried by his sons Esau and Jacob." Meanwhile, Jacob has grown, and taken two wives, Leah and Rachel. Rachel dies in childbirth, as Benjamin is born. Jacob's thirteen children grow into the tribes represented on these windows surrounding us, and their grandmother Rebecca dies, and she is followed by Leah, both buried in Hebron. Jacob survives his mistaken belief that his favorite son Joseph has been torn to death by wild animals, and he lives to see Joseph become the second most powerful man in all of Egypt. Jacob lives in Egypt with his son for seventeen years. When he is 147 years old, he blesses his grandchildren and, breathing his last, is gathered to his people. Joseph dies at 110, is embalmed and placed in a coffin in Egypt. In Exodus, we learn that Joseph died, and all his brothers, and all that generation, but the Israelites multiplied and increased very greatly.

When we are at a distance from our *own* pain and grief, or the fear of it, it is possible to see the flow of life, the rhythm of human existence. One generation comes, one generation goes. The Talmud teaches it directly (Ber. 17a). The end of a human being is death; every creature born must die.

Our tradition teaches us that death is a natural part of life, that death is neither a punishment, nor an evil perpetrated on us, but is part of the intricate structure of human life. Though it be painful,

There is Meaning to be Wrested from Death

the deaths of those we love and, ultimately, our own deaths, are experiences we are intended to have, that are to be thought about and considered, wrestled with and come to terms with, learned from, throughout our lives.

We live in a modern world, however, that has chosen, in the main, to ignore the reality of death. We distance ourselves from it in every way possible, rarely thinking about it, hardly speaking of it. We – who are born into such wealth, such health, so much technology and so many advances in medicine – we have so many chances for life to prevail that we have a hard time grasping that death will indeed prevail, for all of us. We have made death the enemy, because there are now so many ways to beat it back. But by constantly engaging in the struggle to overcome death, we have lost our capacity to embrace death as a meaningful, and a valuable part of life. There are, to be sure, tragic deaths, deaths that interrupt the normal rhythm of life. We know, too, the horror of deaths that come to those too young, deaths that come too fast, accidents, or shootings, or death that doesn't come quickly enough, causing great suffering. But death is not, in and of itself, tragic, or even bad. It is sad, yes, so sad. But we have turned all death into tragedy, out of our fear of looking at it and thinking about it, and facing it.

After experiencing this year of loss, I come to tell you that it is not a coincidence that death is part of our lives. It is not a capricious quirk of nature or a cosmic error that we live our lives within the boundaries of certain death. I believe this reality is part of God's creation, and so, as with everything else God created, there is meaning to be wrested from it.

The wisdom that can come from surviving the death of someone we love is enormous. It cannot come during our anguish, but eventually, it comes. First, we experience the tenderness of a caring community that holds us up as we move through the darkest places. We learn that we matter to so many more people than we might have imagined. We discover that our community is a powerful source of strength, that there is great comfort to be taken from those who are brave enough to witness our mourning.

As we move beyond the worst of the pain, we begin to see that we have grown and changed in ways we never could have imagined. We are challenged to find the answers to remarkable questions: who will I be without so and so? Who must I become now that he or she is gone? What is my life to be about now? We begin to learn what it means to live with and to move beyond great pain. We come to understand, with much greater clarity, what the person who died meant to us.

From the Talmud: Rav died. His disciples traveled to be at his funeral. On the trip back home they stopped and ate a meal by the river Danak. When they were about to say grace, they became involved in a question they could not resolve. Rav Addah bar Ahabah rose and made a second tear in his garment and said: Rav is dead, and we have not yet learned from him even the rules about grace.

So death leads us to so much knowledge: what we hadn't yet learned from the one who died, and all that we *had* learned. All we appreciated about him, and all that we had neglected to appreciate. We learn what in the relationship was truly good and will nurture us as long as we live. And we can acknowledge what was destructive and cannot be allowed to be a part of other relationships, as we come to understand what we had and did not have.

We begin to learn how we will make do with what we have left. There are parts of ourselves that remain undiscovered until we have had to move beyond a loss. Perhaps the adult child who loses a parent learns how to move into being the next generation of the fully adult, grown world. The wife who loses a husband may move into a new journey she never could have known before. The husband who loses a wife may learn to love again, in a new and different way, each ultimately finding their lives enriched in a sustaining, though profoundly different way. The young child who loses a parent is changed forever, with sensibilities and awarenesses she could not have attained any other way. Each time we face a death, we are slammed by the force of the ultimate reality. For an instant, we remember how precious every moment is of the years allotted to us. And though it is impossible to grasp that knowledge day in and day out, a layer of it is laid down in the core of our beings. We are reminded that we do not have forever. Our time is limited. And we don't know how limited. We re-commit ourselves to moving through the difficult times and beyond them, to a place in which we can better cherish the time we have.

On the eve of *Yom Kippur*, thinking seriously of death will force us to ask: What if my spouse died today? Have I said all that needs to be said? How would the relationship be judged if it ended now? Have I given it my best, made it all that it can be? What if my father goes tomorrow, or my mother? What else needed to be asked, understood, forgiven? Could I rest easy, would I have a sense of peace, in mourning those I love? Can I love them as well in this life, as I will love them in death?

Such gains do not justify our losses, or explain them. But they do accompany our grief nonetheless, adding so many layers of understanding to our lives. There is something deeply ennobling about experiencing a death. When we are not immobilized by our grief, we can begin to see that human experience is in so many ways enriched by the existence of death as part of the natural rhythm of life. It raises the stakes, and demands of us that we learn discipline, that we grow and change, and ultimately, that we let go.

This is the irony: in our daily lives, we may view all death as tragedy, so we deny its presence as best as we can, and deprive ourselves of the opportunity to extract its wisdom. But when the death comes, we do the opposite. We *deny* the epic proportions of its tragic effect on us. All of a sudden, we wish not to see the death as an earthquake in our lives that requires all our time and attention and renders it impossible to go on normally. Rather, at this time, we minimize the tragedy of death, as we try to avoid its power, choosing to move through its wake as quickly, and as "normally" as possible.

We adopt the attitude of "keeping a stiff upper lip," and reject the rituals that can pierce our armor and that can insist that we mourn deeply and openly. Some request that the coffin not be lowered into the ground or refuse to place earth on the coffin, rituals that rightly demand the open expression of grief. Some ask about cremation, preferring, in their words, "to keep it simple." In all my years as a rabbi, I can count on one hand the number of people who chose to sit *shiva* for the full seven days. We have things to do, we say; we have to go back to work, we have to take care of the estate, the house. It will be too depressing to sit *shiva* so long. I'll do better if I keep busy.

Jewish tradition points us in a completely different direction. Its awareness of the power of grief and the need to give oneself over to it is so strong, that between the time of the death and the burial itself, one is considered to be in a special state, called *Aninut*. During *Aninut*, a person is understood to be completely overcome by grief, to move in a devastated fog of black despair. So, during this time, nothing is expected of the mourner. He is to be brought meals, as he cannot be expected to provide for himself. He is relieved of the obligations of all *mitzvot*, in the traditional system, even of the obligation to pray three times a day. The grief is understood to be overwhelming, and the mourner is expected to give in to it.

For a while. For, one is expected to be present for the burial. And at that time, one moves to the second stage, called *Avelut*. No longer permitted to be wild in her grief, the mourner is expected to bear the funeral and to recite *Kaddish*. All expressions of grief are encouraged. She should cry, tear the collar of her garment or a *kria* ribbon, weep and grieve, and not be ashamed to do so; but she is expected to move through the rituals, to return home, to sit and be surrounded by those coming to pay a *shiva* call, to cope.

For seven days, the mourner is to sit with the grief, to let it flow in and out of his mind and heart, to tell stories, to look at pictures, to live in a protected space, a space outside of time, in which one's grief is inhabited, fully, deeply. On the seventh day, the mourners rise from their *shiva*. Traditionally, they take a walk around the block to ritually end *shiva*, as a symbol of their return to normal life. For the first thirty days, *shloshim*, there are different rules. One may go to work, but avoids parties and merriment. One is considered a mourner for an entire year, until, after the first *yahrtzeit*, one moves out of the category of mourner, and is expected to embrace life, once again.

Today we short-circuit the cycle of grieving, even as we avoid thinking about death, before the experience of it is thrust upon us. With both actions we choose the modern culture's denial of death, rather than the Jewish tradition's acceptance of it. Don't be afraid, our tradition teaches us. Or, be afraid, and then find the courage to plumb the depths of the reality of death. Move through the sadness it brings, and then force your mind and heart to engage the wisdom it teaches. Knowing that death will come to all of us, and to all those we love, bravely wrestle with it and learn from it, learn – how to live, and perhaps grow wise enough to learn – how to die.

Of all the ancient texts of our tradition, the 23rd Psalm may be the most familiar. "The Lord is my Shepherd, I shall not want." Generation after generation has memorized it, its words are hallowed, their sharp edges softened by the lips and souls of so many who have recited it. "Yea, though I walk through the valley of the shadow of death, I will fear no evil," we mumble – in a moment of fear – or recite in a hospital corridor, waiting, or sing at a funeral, or hold quietly in our hearts in any moment of temptation or fear, or sadness. "I shall not fear, for You are with me." The secret wisdom has been passed down, parent to child, preacher to seeker. Somehow, it is all part of the plan, and somehow, we will divine its meaning. I love this psalm because it is not only for funerals and for grieving, but it is also for those moments of triumph, when we catch a glimpse of the holiness that brings us to say: this too, has meaning.

Surely goodness and mercy shall follow me all the days of my life, and I shall dwell in the house of the Lord forever.

A LETTER TO GOD ABOUT DEATH

Dear God,

It's time we talked about it. We've had so many deaths this year, and I need to talk to you about it. You know, we did last year, too, and I gave a sermon about death last *Yom Kippur*. My colleagues kid me that I'm going to become known as the "death rabbi," if every year I write this kind of a sermon, but it is the only thing that really matters, isn't it? Death . . . and what it helps us know about living.

Remember, it was death that brought me to you, and the rabbinate in the first place. When my father died you were so present to me, in the words my rabbi spoke, when I cut the *kria* ribbon and felt the tear in my heart, in the faces of all the people who came to say *Kaddish* with us, in every platter of food they brought. I was thirteen years old and I knew you were there – even as Psalm 22 became my favorite Psalm: "Oh God, my God, why have you forsaken me?" That was the essence of it – feeling forsaken by you and embraced by you at the same time. I couldn't imagine how we would all go on and yet you carried us somehow, on eagles' wings.

Now, almost exactly thirty years later, I am beginning to understand how.

Kalmen died this year, God, maybe the perfect death, at a hundred years old, with so much good living to his credit. But he's gone, and we miss him so. David Cohen died and we hear his wisdom ringing in our ears. Little Rebecca died, only four years old – I'll have more to say to you about that one. Roger died, leaving six-year old Dory, and Claire's mother and sister-in-law died, in the space of two weeks. Did it have to be so hard on her brother, to lose his wife when he'd barely started grieving for his mother? My cousin Susan died, 48, cancer. Maybe I *am* the "death rabbi" . . . in all the anger and sadness, I stand witness to your presence, I sense you permeating it all. But it's hard, God, so hard. Did you have to make the system so hard on us, mere human beings?

Do you remember that address book I had as a kid? I kept it for years and every now and then would turn its pages, remembering friends who had come and gone. There was a poem printed on the back inside cover that always amused me, for it seemed so trite and silly. I don't remember the words exactly, but it had to do with some man who meant to be in touch with his old buddy, and never quite got around to it. He thought to call, tried to write, but somehow he always got too busy. Finally one year, he got the number, made the call . . . only to be told that his friend had just died a few months before. Do you know I literally laughed at how absurd and contrived that was? Now I know, God, now I know; it's not absurd, not contrived, but the absolute truth.

A Letter to God About Death

Yom Kippur reminds us: it could all be over, any time. There is no guarantee of even one more minute.

I've been reading Hemingway this year, God. He says, "How can we live, seeing we have to die?" He's got it all wrong, doesn't he? I looked for you in his thoughts . . . and didn't find you there. You would turn that thought on its head and teach: Seeing we have to die, must we not live? Must we not live every moment, every action, every choice, with gusto, with awareness, with intensity? It is knowing that our lives are finite, truly accepting, in the deepest part of our beings, that there are only a certain number of days allotted to us, that makes our living really matter. It is the sure knowledge of death's coming that urges us to live fully.

Well, you know, I've always needed a deadline to produce anything. Now I've finally got it, God; very funny – a *dead*-line, so that we will produce a life. So then, death is not the enemy – it is the opportunity. Perhaps we never truly live until we discipline ourselves to face the truth that we will die.

But you know, God, I wanted to tell you: people don't think about these things very much. It's too frightening. I know you didn't mean it to be that way, but we are not so strong as you imagined us to be. It's very hard for us, God, to think about the end of our own lives, even though that's exactly what keeps us aware of just how precious life is. How is it that it takes us half of life to come to the knowledge, that each moment of it is precious?

Ah, I have a new metaphor, God, for expressing this problem. Maybe you heard it when I premiered it in the Intro to Judaism class. It's somewhat inelegant, but the more I work with it, the more powerful it becomes to me. Okay, here goes. Life, God, is like a tube of toothpaste. Okay, just go with me here. At first, you have a whole, smooth tube in your hand, full, fresh, unbroken. Without even thinking about it, you push down and squeeze out as much as you wish, or more – it doesn't matter. You squeeze until, after some time, you realize you are getting towards the end of the tube. You're not sure whether there's another one in the drawer and you have to make it last, and you begin to squeeze out just enough each time, hoping you'll have enough for tonight, for tomorrow morning – and it suddenly seems so precious. (By the way, to extend the metaphor a bit, it would have been nice to know, with certainty, that there was another tube in the drawer, God, but I can see that, from your perspective, that would have compromised the beauty of the whole system. Not knowing forces us to focus on what we have in this life and still leaves us hopeful about what might be.)

So every morning, I squeeze that tube and, Oh God, I know how precious each moment, each day, of this life is. But here's the thing, God: as precious as it is, day-to-day living can be so . . . irritating . . . and trivial . . . and difficult. It's unrelenting, God, the things you have to do, the problems you have to take care of. It's all so precious, sure, until the frustration of the moment makes you lose your temper, and all of a sudden you're cross, or yelling your head off. Every moment is precious, we know, until you're doing some brain-numbing, repetitive activity that makes you want to scream. Every bit of it is precious, God, until you're so lonely or tired, or angry, that you lose perspective entirely, and you just want this particular time to be past. That's what it is to be human, God; it's quite a challenge to always see the big picture, to keep that *dead*-line in mind.

Did you know this idea of "multi-tasking" would come up? That it would be viewed as a healthy strategy to do three or four things at the same time? Or road rage? That's one that will help you lose the sense of life's being precious, just like the snap of your fingers. Have people always felt compelled to work so hard? Did it surprise you when people started to be competitive about how busy they are, and about how tired they are? Okay, so the way we live our lives is the result of our choices, not yours, but you have to admit that, as amazing as the system is, there are some kinks in it. Did you predict how enormous the challenge would be for us to truly be present in the moment, to take our awareness of the deadline into each moment, so that we could make it as meaningful as possible? Whew, it's hard, God. Many moments in this life are hard.

We lean on you, you know, to help us remember that we are stringing those memories into a lifetime, and that the lifetime is precious. Help us take the long view, God, and help us be calm.

So you gave me a new experience this year God. *Shechechiyanu, v'kiyimanu, v'higianu, lazman, hazeh*. For the first time in my life, I watched a person die. It was a very moving, and strangely life-giving sight. You were there, I know you were, but let me tell you what it was like from my perspective. He had had such a hard time, God; he was struggling to breathe. We couldn't tell how much pain he was in, but we knew he was working hard to move through those last moments. Do you remember? He opened his eyes at the last, as if to say good-byes, as if to acknowledge the good-byes being said to him. Then he drew those last, few, soul-wrenching breaths . . . and was still. I understood in that moment why "breath" and "spirit" are the same word in Hebrew, *ruach*. When his breath finally stopped, it was clear that all of who he was, was gone; it was just gone somehow. And we were left with this very precious casing, his body, but all of who he was, was gone. I blessed his body, you know, with the familiar words: "May God bless you and keep you . . ." but his soul was . . . where,

God? Where was his soul, his essence? We hope and pray, it was on some other plane of existence that we cannot yet perceive – but God, he sure was gone from *this* existence. It helps us, you know, to actually witness the going; it helps us break through the denial and recall . . . the *dead*-line.

But God, did you have to make it so hard? Must people fight their way out of this life? I know that sometimes we make it worse, in our demand for every last minute. With our respirators and our feeding tubes we make it harder for people to die and then we lay it at your feet, but you have a part in this, too, you know. Couldn't we all die peacefully, in our sleep?

And while I'm being angry, is there any sense we are supposed to make out of the death by cancer of a four-year old girl? So much pain, God, so much sadness. I'm sure we learned from it, but at what cost? Did the system have to be so cruel? Are we making it more cruel, with all our modern inventions that poison the food we eat and the air we breathe? It's the hardest stretch for me to make, God, and I'm stretching as hard as I can, to believe that your magnificent system of limited days in a human life requires all these variations in death, that all these different kinds of deaths at different ages are somehow necessary for us to learn, to progress.

The stretching is making me more flexible, though, with each passing death, as I see noble human beings square their shoulders, carry the burden, and move forward. I do believe that it is by your grace that we are ultimately so strong, and that by your grace the system, ultimately, works with all the kinks still in it. Perhaps you could work on it a bit, God, from your side, because I can tell you, we human beings are working hard at grasping its meaning, from our side.

A Letter to God About Death

I have a new favorite Psalm, God, Psalm 90: "Like grass we flourish for a day. By nightfall we fade and wither." No more "why have you abandoned me, O God?" I am, instead, working on acceptance. "Three score and ten our years may number" – do you know how long it took me to realize that was 70? – "four score if granted the vigor. Life quickly passes and flies away. So teach us to use all our days, that we may attain a heart of wisdom."

Teach us, God, that life is a blessing, all the more so because it is strictly limited. Help us be aware of that every single, precious moment. Oh God, help us to live. Help us . . . to truly live.

Sincerely,
Carole L. Meyers

SUICIDE

Saul was the first king of Israel, some 3,000 years ago. He was handsome, spiritual, modest, a charismatic leader. His great heroism on the battlefield was known throughout the world. Saul had it all; he was the golden boy.

But there is another way of understanding King Saul. There was a Saul who was driven by tremendous conflicts in his life, with Samuel, the prophet who anointed him king, and with the young and challenging David, who would become king after him. His rift with Samuel caused him to lose faith in himself; his fear of David's growing popularity made him constantly suspicious. It all darkened Saul's mind. One commentator writes that it is easy to see Saul's life begin to take a tragic course, alternating fits of hatred and love, violence and depression.

Finally, on a battlefield, surrounded by his enemies, despairing of his own fate, King Saul chose to kill himself, falling on his own sword.

Suicide

Perhaps it was a soldier's death, as our tradition likes to say, arguing that he killed himself, knowing fully that if he did not, the Philistines would do so, momentarily, in a torturous, degrading way. But perhaps Saul was more like us, more like the many people we all know, who have, at one time or another, thought of killing themselves, tried to kill themselves, and like the ones who *have* killed themselves. Saul had had more than his share of pain and depression.

Research tells us that the idea that only psychotic, or "crazy" people kill themselves is patently false. It's estimated that less than 15% of people who kill themselves can be diagnosed this way. The rest were diagnosed as depressed, and there is nothing rare about depression; as much as 80% of the U.S. population will eventually suffer from various degrees of depression – loneliness, feelings of hopelessness, and despair.

Here are the facts: in 1987, the last year for which figures are available, 30,796 Americans took their own lives. On an average day, 1,000 people kill themselves worldwide. Since the 1950's, the adolescent suicide rate in the United States has climbed 300%.

But we don't need to hear statistics to know the breadth of that reality in our lives. Some of us are experiencing the excruciating pain of surviving the suicide of someone we loved; others care deeply for someone who is a survivor. More of us know and care for people who have thought or talked seriously about suicide and who have, perhaps, attempted it. Most, if not all of us, have, at one time or another, thought, however abstractly, about killing ourselves.

Suicide is very present in our times. It is touching all of our lives, in one way or another, but we are not talking about it. And on this one thing, all the experts agree: the best thing we can do about suicide, is to talk about it. In every situation related to suicide – with people who are survivors of the suicide, with an attempted suicide of a loved one, with people who themselves are tempted by suicide – we need to talk, to articulate the unspoken, to speak about what seems unspeakable. When better to do so, than on *Kol Nidre* night, when there is to be no pretense, when we struggle to let our defenses down? When better to break the silence, and begin to say the words: She killed herself; he killed himself, I think about killing myself . . . words and words, talk and more talk, until there is some lifting, some lightening, some understanding, even if it is only temporary, even if it will require many more words, before the talking is done.

I want to address, briefly, these three different groups. First, it is said that a person who commits suicide leaves his or her skeleton in every survivor's closet, causing immense pain. One survivor has said that learning to cope with this daily pain is like an arthritis patient learning to cope with the agony of movement. We need to know that our fear and unwillingness to speak openly about suicide causes the survivors to become further victimized. One woman who lost her son gives us some insight. "I used to drive down the street thinking I had a sign on my car that said, 'MY SON KILLED HIMSELF.' Another car would pass me and I would think, 'Now they know.'" A woman who lost her 16-year old daughter says: "Losing her was painful enough, but the whispers, feeling like a leper, being avoided, having people act like nothing happened, never mentioning the death, is almost worse."

The best thing we can do with a survivor of a suicide is to talk with him or her, to initiate conversation, to create an atmosphere in which a sense of shame is diminished, and replaced by openness and understanding. We need to be brave enough to talk.

Second, the director of the Suicide Prevention Center of Los Angeles was recently quoted as saying: "Let's face it. Everybody thinks about suicide. Anybody who says he hasn't is lying." The best thing we can do when we are tempted by suicide is to talk about it, to take our own depression seriously, and to get help. One woman who attempted to kill herself, and failed, talks about her state of mind. "I had tunnel vision. Unable to sleep, for countless nights, I withheld endlessly, seeking a solution. I felt that I had logically evaluated every alternative, but could find no other solution. I had to die. In reality, I was in deep clinical depression, which could have been, and finally was, treated." We need to be brave enough to break out of our tunnel vision, to confide in someone else, to talk.

Third, I address myself, with the same message, to all of us who one day may be able to have an effect on someone who is contemplating suicide. Talk with them, day and night, if you have to. One of the great myths about suicide is that nothing could have stopped her, once she decided to kill herself. Even the most hopelessly suicidal person has mixed emotions about death, wavering until the very last moment between wanting death and desperately wanting life. Another myth is that talking about suicide to a troubled person may give the person morbid ideas. People are concerned about this especially with adolescents, where the suicide rate is so high. The truth is, you don't give a suicidal person ideas about suicide; he or she already has them. Talking about them will help to bring them into the open where they can be dealt with honestly and directly. Far from being dangerous to talk about suicide, it is dangerous not to talk about it. A further myth is that suicides often occur out of the blue. It is more likely instead that family and friends have been too distracted to see the hints, the threats, the terminal misery. Suicide is usually a response to a long, deep depression, which we have to be open enough to see and, again, brave enough to talk about.

Leaning on God

What does Judaism have to say about all this? Most of you would guess the traditional view of suicide, that it is a *chet*, a sin, that the person committing suicide should be buried at the far edges of the cemetery, and that no mourning rituals are to be observed. In reality, the attitude is much different. These rules are meant to dissuade one from suicide, but, after the fact, an extremely rigorous definition of suicide is routinely applied, so that almost no death can be defined legally as suicide. This attitude allows individual rabbis and communities to respond to these deaths in a much more humane way, as they see fit. The attitude is one of deepest sadness, not judgment; the desire is to mourn, but not to eulogize. Rabbi Akiva said: "Although the man who committed suicide may be pardoned, he should not be praised as an example. He should be, quietly, forgiven."

Nor would you be surprised at the positive statement of Judaism's attitude about all this: that we are commanded to teach and to emphasize the value and holiness of life as a God-given gift, to be held in sacred trust. It is dicey to suggest this, in the face of those whose despair is leading them towards suicide. It is dicier still, to say that every blessing, every holiday, every tradition of Judaism struggles to reach this sacredness of life, yet it is so. Every element of Jewish life tries to infuse meaning and hope.

The great symbol of this hope is Elijah the prophet, *Eliyahu ha-navi*, the one you know from Passover and Havdalah. There are hundreds of Elijah stores, filled with hope and the clear sense that "This too, will pass." They are secret stories, sometimes saccharine, usually simplistic. Take the story of the two neighbors, one woman poor, but happy; the other rich, but miserable. Before Pesach, each woman takes her children's clothes to the river to be washed. Each woman is greeted by an old man. The poor woman tells him that the tears in her eyes are caused only by soap suds, when in fact, she is masking her sadness at the meager festival they will have. Yet she tells him they are prepared for Pesach, with wine and matzah, candles and tablecloth. The rich woman simply grumbles about all her hard wash, her angers and her bitterness about her good-for-nothing husband and her lot in life.

On the evening of Pesach, the poor woman's table is meager indeed, but she cheerfully and lovingly begins to read the Hagadah. In the rich woman's house, there is much on the table, but only complaints and arguments are heard.

The old man is said to have knocked on each of their doors, telling them that the words they spoke on the banks of the river would come true. And so it was. In the rich woman's house, there was continued bickering and unhappiness. In the poor woman's house, there was suddenly everything a person could want: silver candlesticks, a magnificent meal, light, happiness and love.

The story ends by saying that the poor woman wanted to thank the man who brought such miracles, but he had disappeared, and was never seen again. Then she knew that he was *Eliyahu ha-navi* and the legend of Elijah's ability to plant seeds of hope and faith was born.

On the face of it, such a story could be quite insensitive to one in pain. But think of the people who told these stories; their lives were filled with misery and despair, with poverty and persecutions and blood libels. These tales of miracles brought them hope. They knew they weren't true, just as we know they aren't. But the human soul craves hope, and in our tradition it finds that hope in small increments, in songs and stories, in *Eliyahu ha-navi*, in blessings, and festivals, in this festival of *Yom Kippur*.

This day of *Yom Kippur* is about dying. It is about facing the forces that are leading us toward death, when we are still alive. It is about facing what we hate about ourselves and about our lives, and it is about believing that change is possible.

This is the day we do not eat, we do not drink, we are prohibited from sexual relations. We traditionally wear white – some say to remind us of the shroud, others say to remind us that we have the capacity to be angels. Either way, it is as if we ourselves are being held in the balance between life and death, for twenty-four hours, as we abstain from these life-affirming behaviors. But the whole experience is meant to make us see that we do not wish to be dead, in our bodies or in our souls.

We wish to find a way to live. May we find it, may we be blessed to help others find it, may 5752 be a year of hope and faith, a year in which the presence of *Eliyahu ha-navi* makes our hearts grow strong.

May it be God's will.

REACTING TO EVIL: THE LESSON OF JOB

I have been reading the book of Job. It is not a part of the Bible we tend to read very often. We read from the Torah, the first section of the Bible, weekly, and we comment upon it often. The second section of the Bible, the Prophets, we read less often, but we do hear the visions and dreams of Isaiah, Ezekiel, and Jeremiah when a haftarah portion is read. But the third section of the Bible, called the Writings, which is where the book of Job is, we look at far less often. Ecclesiastes is read on *Succot*, Ruth on *Shavuot*, but some others, like Job, could go without compelling our attention for a long time. Besides, Job has the reputation of being a troubling book; it requires that we grapple with Job's unjust suffering and try to make some sense out of it and our own lives. It is not hard to see why we do not naturally pick this book up for a good read.

But that is just what I've found myself doing these past few days. Someone remarked to me that our congregation has seen more than its share of sadness over the last few years than there seemed to have been in the past. I think she was right; it may be that our congregation is naturally reaching the end of a cycle, for its builders are older and more tired, or it may be just sad coincidence. We do not know why, but we do know the experience of loss.

And although we tend to forget it, Job is, when all is said and done, a comforting book, an inspiring book. So I have been reading Job.

Years ago, I had always thought of the book as kind of a problem. Poor Job is the most upright, virtuous man around, and yet he becomes a pawn in a game played between God and Satan.

Most scholars agree that the book of Job was written somewhere between the years 600 and 400 B.C.E. At this time, the word Satan had no associations with devils or demons or hell. Satan was not understood to be the opposite of God, but part of God, the antagonist, the one who challenges and argues and dares God. The Hebrew word Satan is not left as "Satan," in good English translations, but is translated as "Adversary." Only against the background of the Christian world, between the years 200 and 500 C.E. did the idea of Satan as the devil enter Jewish literature.

So in the story of Job, the Adversary dares God to put his most faithful servant to the test. He wants to prove that not even a perfect man could remain true to God in the face of unexplained, terrible, suffering. God agrees to the test, and the most horrible tortures begin to afflict Job. He loses his property and his livelihood. His sons and daughters all die. He develops every kind of painful illness imaginable. In all of his pain, Job sits with three friends who come to comfort him. In nearly forty chapters of dialogue, they spout the conventional

Reacting to Evil: The Lesson of Job

wisdom of their world. They tell Job two main things: first, that God's actions are always understandable; God rewards good people and punishes evil people. Second, therefore, if Job will simply confess his wrongdoings and repent, his sufferings will cease.

These pieces of wisdom were common to early Israelite religion. And although Job disagrees with them, as we do, he really has no new ideas of his own to substitute for them. Or at least it appears that way on the surface.

In reality, I see in two simple statements Job makes, an entirely different perspective on how to react to evil. First, Job has the wisdom to ask the following question: "Should we accept only good from God and not evil?" He knows what the rules of the game are. He knows that to be alive is to deal with whatever comes along, both good and evil. He knows better than to make the assumption that only good is supposed to come. Evil is part of the picture too. Even though an understanding of why evil affects us is beyond us, Job refuses to allow the existence of evil to undermine the goodness and the aliveness of life.

So many of us tend not to think about God very much at all, until a tragedy comes along, until we feel wronged. Then we are quick to blame God, to express all our anger: How dare you let this happen to me? Why me? Job knew that to blame God for the evil in our lives is to attribute to God a power that must be the cause of the goodness in our lives as well. "Shall I accept good from God and not evil?" Job is wise enough and strong enough to affirm God and goodness in the face of evil.

Secondly, Job never stops insisting that he was innocent of any wrongdoing. His friends, his family, his wife beg him to repent, to end his transgressions, to deserve goodness from God, not evil. Job continues to deny their accusations. He says to God: "I am blameless.

Relent. Let there not be injustice. Relent! I am still in the right." Job refuses to give in to his society's view that, if he is suffering, it must be the result of his own evil-doing. Instead he had the courage to not blame himself for the evil that befell him. He did not add a heavy load of guilt to the weight of the troubles he was carrying already.

We are often not so easy on ourselves. We are much more likely to take the blame even when it is unjustified. "I must have done something wrong . . . it is my fault . . . I must be a terrible person for this to have happened." Our taking on guilt so easily is another way of grasping at straws. It gives us a reason for the evil we experience, but it is usually the wrong reason. There is evil and sadness and pain in our lives that we do not cause; it is separate from us, and we must not take the blame for it.

The other morning I found myself sitting in front of the television set watching Phil Donahue. It was one of his very sad shows, about parents whose children have been abducted, and the pain they are suffering as they dedicate their lives to searching for these children. One woman said: "You know, it's really true that God works in mysterious ways, and some day we are going to understand the reason for all this." She was waiting, hopelessly I think, for the answer.

Another mother said, "There is no answer. There is only every morning, waking up and realizing all over again, that this is reality. There is no answer; there is only life." In this woman's view, there is still life waiting to be lived.

Ultimately, the Adversary lost his wager. In the end the righteous man, Job, kept his faith in God, and was rewarded, with a new family and with great wealth.

I used to think the Book of Job was something less than comforting for that very reason – how few of us are so generously rewarded for the suffering we experience in our lives. But there is comfort in Job's understanding that life offers both good and evil, and neither without the other. There is comfort in Job's unshakeable knowledge that we are not to blame for our suffering, and must not allow ourselves perversely to take on guilt that we do not deserve.

It is comforting to think that, like Job, we are just human beings who live our lives as best as we can, good and evil, right and wrong, happy and sad, affirming our lives in the face of all kinds of evil, simply by getting out of bed each morning. It is comforting to read Job, to know that throughout the generations, the righteous have often suffered alongside the wicked. It is comforting, finally, to know that our generation continues the struggle to understand why, and continues also, the struggle to accept life as it is, as the gift of God.

THE WORLD IS VERY DANGEROUS

We sit and stare at our television sets in disbelief. ValueJet flight 592 plunged into the Everglades after take-off from Miami International Airport, killing everyone aboard, 104 passengers and 5 crew. For weeks, we read of the slow and dangerous recovery of bodies and possessions.

TWA flight 800 burst into flames and fell into the sea, off the coast of New York. We mourned for 230 random victims who lost their lives. We are bombarded with penetratingly painful information about them: the 16 French club high school students from Pennsylvania; the Los Angeles family of four traveling to Israel for a bar mitzvah; the knowledge of a diamond engagement ring intended to be presented to the prospective bride on holiday outside Paris, now lying at the bottom of the Atlantic Ocean along with the prospective groom.

The World is Very Dangerous

How many times did we watch videos of the commotion surrounding the explosion of a homemade pipe bomb in Atlanta's Centennial Olympic Park. Listening to brave proclamations that "the games will go on," we were stunned by the death of Alice S. Hawthorne, 44 years old, and by the count of 111 people wounded in the explosion.

We have spent so many hours absorbing horrific events that hit so close to home. We realize: It could have been us; it could have been someone we love. And we are afraid. One hundred and sixty eight people died in the Oklahoma City attack. Many of us will see forever, in our mind's eye, the faces of the firemen, carrying the charred babies. And we weep.

We have faced the Unabomber and the death of Polly Klaas. We have seen madmen shooting rifles in post offices and in schools. We patiently endure once-irritating security procedures; we lock our doors; we don't let working people in without seeing their I.D.'s; we don't leave our children alone for an instant. Every time we turn the radio on for the news, we tense, expecting another tragedy; we fear more danger to confront and absorb. Suddenly it seems clear: our world is a dangerous place. We fear for our safety, for the safety of all we love, for the safety of the American people. How shall we respond? How can we understand the danger and our fear, and react to it? How shall we calm and comfort ourselves, in their shadow?

I have three thoughts to share with you about this, this *Yom Kippur* Eve, this sacred time in which we strive to shape the attitudes that will inform our lives throughout the New Year.

The first is that, while there are elements of this danger that are new, and particular to the technological advances of our times, a deeper look shows that the world always has been a dangerous place, filled with conditions that can so easily bring harm to fragile human beings. It is true that the development of automatic weapons and compact, electronically-detonated explosives have given terrorists a new mobility and lethality, and the randomness of their victims makes it seem that the innocent bystander faces greater risk. Yet we know that the world has been filled with terrorism since the ancient Greek historian Xenophon wrote of its effectiveness in the 4th century, B.C. We know of vicious and blanket cruelty, used against whole populations by Roman emperors Tiberius and Caligula, to discourage opposition to their rule. And we know of others: the Spanish Inquisition in the 15th century; Robespierre's reign of terror during the French revolution; the vicious acts of the Ku Klux Klan, originally founded following the Civil War to intimidate supporters of Reconstruction; the unspeakable atrocities of Nazi Germany; countless murders of innocent Russians, under Stalin's rule. Human beings have found ways of brutalizing and endangering other human beings from time immemorial.

As we struggle with the tragedy of AIDS, it is helpful to remember that in the 14th Century, perhaps as much as fifty or sixty per cent of the entire population of Europe and Asia died of the plague. As we face cancer and heart disease, should we not remember that life expectancy has lengthened from as little as fifteen years, in pre-civilization, to twenty-five years in Roman times, to fifty years in 1900, to between seventy-five and eighty years in our time. Throughout most of history, it was a miracle in itself to survive from birth through childhood, given the toll taken by infectious diseases such as smallpox, measles, and cholera.

I think of the tragic kidnapping and murder of the two-year old son of Charles Lindberg, which traumatized America in 1932; of the

The World is Very Dangerous

murders committed by Jack the Ripper in England in the nineteenth century; and of the persons completely unjustifiably and randomly tortured and killed in the witch hunts of Salem, Massachusetts in 1692. Every age, every decade, has brought its own peculiar version of threat to the lives of innocent human beings. In this sense, our age is no different.

Perhaps we are struggling so with this new evidence of threat all around us, because most of us were raised to expect something different, shaped as we were by the Fifties, the decade of *Ozzie & Harriet* and *Leave It To Beaver*. Everything seemed so safe, orderly and prosperous, especially as television appeared in so many of our households, presenting its sanitized version of daily life. Although in our communal memory we maintain this image of the secure, optimistic Fifties, that decade in fact knew its threats as well. Reeling from the moral implications of the use of the atomic bomb, our leaders struggled with the decision to pursue the prediction of the much more powerful hydrogen bomb. At this time, Albert Einstein was asked how the third world war would be fought. He answered glumly that he had no idea what kind of weapons would be used, but he could assure the questioner that the war after that would be fought with stones. In the Fifties, we faced the possibility of the most devastating destruction imaginable. School children were regularly drilled in safety procedures for use in case of a bombing – procedures that we knew could not make them safe. Into this uncertain time raged Senator Joseph McCarthy on a four-year spree of accusations, charges, and threats that left many Americans devastated spiritually, financially and emotionally.

On this *Kol Nidre* night, when we value brutal honesty above all else, we know that human life always has been threatened, by war and political instability, by natural disasters, by the evil of human beings. Our vulnerability is not quantitatively different.

What do we do? How do we respond to the fear and the pain? My second thought is a deceptively simple one. In the words of Professor of Religion Martin Marty, people begin by coping. It sounds so simplistic, so Pollyana-ish. But his answer represents a reality that transcends the generations. People have an immense capacity to absorb the pain and loss inevitably present in human life. We have wells of strength that run so deep. We are strong enough to face exploding planes, terrorist bombs, and even the devastation caused by a personal crisis in our lives. We are strong. And we can cope. We do cope, so much more, so much better, than we could possibly have imagined before a loss occurs. I take comfort in the words of Dr. Marty: "Faith is born and survives in a world where serious people make their lifelong affirmations, while fully aware of the chaos within them, the random around them, and the threatening before them."*

People begin by coping. And, more often than not, ultimately, we do cope.

A story is told by my colleague Jack Reimer about the violinist Itzhak Perlman, who came on stage to give a concert at Lincoln Center. A survivor of childhood polio, Perlman makes his way across a stage using crutches, slowly sits and unclasps his leg braces, and pulls up one foot and then the other. He places his violin under his chin, nods to the conductor, and gets ready to play.

This is the usual routine. But this time, the story goes, just as he finished the first few bars, one of the strings on his violin snapped, like gunfire across the room. So the maestro either had to get another

---

*Marty, Martin E. "When Meaning Eludes Us." *Los Angeles Times*, July 28, 1996. Web.

violin or replace the string, and either choice would involve the laborious and painful process of re-clasping braces, slowly leaving and returning, re-seating himself, unclasping the braces, and preparing anew to begin.

But he didn't. Instead, he waited a moment, closed his eyes, and signaled the conductor to begin again. The orchestra began, and he played from where he had left off. Music aficionados know that it is difficult, perhaps impossible, to play a symphonic work with just three strings. But Itzhak Perlman refused to know that, and played on, adjusting and re-adjusting, and finishing the piece. Silence first greeted the conclusion, then screaming and cheering for this magnificent performance.

Perlman raised his bow to quiet the crowd and said "You know, sometimes it is the artist's task to find out how much music you can make, with what you have left." So the story goes.

People begin by coping. And in our coping with what we sometimes have, we create miraculous music.

It is this miraculous music that is the substance of my third thought. In addition to all the danger and evil surrounding us, there *is* goodness as well. Most of us cannot see it for the simple reason that we are up so close to it; it surrounds us day by day. The fish is not conscious of the water in which it swims; the water just is.

Only when we can pull back, and see with the perspective of distance, does that which surrounds us become visible. From a distance we can see: the miraculous, intricate workings of the human body, which day by day do not fail us; the outreaching hand of another human being, pulling us over a hurdle; the warmth of the sun, nourishing our bodies and our hearts; the sweetness of a newborn child bringing new hope for life. Our tradition teaches that the

Shechinah, the in-dwelling presence of God, is all around us, all the time, if we could only train ourselves to perceive it, to be constantly aware. Moreover, we have the power to embody the *Shechinah*, in the acts we choose to do, in the words we say, in our ability to connect with other human beings and to recognize God in them. All around us is *Shechinah*. All around us is *Shechinah*.

We are so quick to blame God for all the evil, yet so slow to perceive God's goodness. We rage against God for allowing the evil of the Holocaust; yet do we even notice the miracle of Hitler's defeat in World War II? I learned from recently reading the journalist Howard K. Smith that the Allied victory was *hardly* inevitable, that in the fall of 1940, Britain was nearly decimated, Russia intimidated, and America experiencing a strong current of anti-war thinking. In that same year, the American draft passed by a single vote. God is as present in the courage and perseverance of decent people who differentiated good from evil and took unpopular stances which, in the end, caused Hitler's defeat, as God is to blame for the evils perpetrated in the Holocaust.

All around us is *Shechinah*.

Even there, even in the horror of horrors we name the Holocaust, God's presence is to be found, argues our wise Rabbi Harold Schulweis. In his new book, *For Those Who Can't Believe*, he recounts the many tales he has personally documented, of the indescribable courage and goodness of those who risked all to save Jews. There were tens of thousands of them, I was surprised to learn, who forged passports, falsified baptismal certificates, organized underground safety and escape routes. There were thousands who hid Jews in their homes, when to offer a Jew food, drink, or shelter was a capital crime. Rabbi Schulweis relates events that took place in Poland, in Germany, in Dutch villages and in the French countryside, in Bulgaria, in Finland, in Italy. Rabbi Shulweis teaches: "[i]n every land occupied by the Nazis, there were persons who would not feign blindness and muteness."*

All around us is *Shechinah*. I do not presume to present a theological justification for the Holocaust. But what I know, what comforts and instructs, is that *even* there, goodness, the presence of the *Shechinah*, was possible.

We begin to transcend the tragedies we experience, and we learn to quiet our fears, by forcing ourselves to see, to fully apprehend the goodness that does exist all around us in our day-to-day lives, and in the miraculous acts of goodness even contained within horrible evil. We discipline ourselves to a constant awareness of the *Shechinah*, of God's presence surrounding us in nature *and* in human action.

We battle our fear by *knowing* that all around us is *Shechinah*, God's in-dwelling presence in the world, which supports us, holds us up, gives us strength, when we have the faith to lean on it.

Think back to when you heard about the Oklahoma City bombing, or the explosion of TWA flight 800. First we felt the horror of it, then the sadness, then the fear; but before we settled into the fear, there was a moment for many of us, when relief swept over us, as we realized that we were safe, that the people we love were safe. And no matter how bad a day we had been having, life was suddenly suffused with meaning, and we knew how precious this life is. In our tradition we call this awareness *Yirat Shamayim*, reverence for creation. Feeling it does not justify the evil, or mitigate the danger,

---

* Schulweis, Harold M., *For Those Who Can't Believe: Overcoming the Obstacles to Faith.* New York: Harper Collins, 1994. P. 150.

but it is a brilliant reminder to us that our passion for life, our energy for it, our commitment to it, is *so* strong, just below the surface of our fear, that we are convinced we *will* find the strength to persevere, in the face of all the fear, and the evil, as generations before us have done.

We remember the strength of those who preceded us; it gives us the courage to cope, and we will ourselves to see the goodness, surrounding us, as clearly as we are forced to see the evil.

And, we move forward.

EVIL AND FAITH

The hardest thing I have ever done in my Rabbinate was the funeral of a four-month old boy. His parents were congregants of mine whom I was extremely fond of. I had officiated at his mother's conversion and at his baby-naming. Four months later, Daniel was willfully and maliciously murdered by his babysitter. It was the most extreme kind of tragedy I could imagine: a horrible, brutal act inflicted on an innocent and helpless human being.

What I have come to know since that funeral is that tragedy of this dimension is not so unusual in our world, but is instead an all too real experience. It may be one little infant girl who survives an airplane crash, in which the rest of her family dies, or three young brothers who have contracted the AIDS virus from blood transfusions required because they were hemophiliacs, or any of a variety of headlines that appear in our daily newspapers. There are endless possibilities: the early death of a parent, sexual abuse of a child, drunk driving accidents. Sometimes it seems that tragedy itself is the norm and the unusual thing, the blessing to be thankful for, is uninterrupted, normal life.

And there is tragedy of a more subtle variety. In a stirringly real television mini-series, a recently widowed father and his grown daughter sit, staring into space, in a dimly-lit family room. The daughter says: "I'm thirty-five years old, divorced twice, moving back home with my two children. It's not exactly the life I'd imagined for myself." And her father responds: "It never is." There is the tragedy of absorbing the shock of reality, reality which seems to fall so short of our childhood visions.

Perhaps the amazing thing is that we continue to be so shocked. We continue to expect life to be fair, generous and comprehensible. And it is not. And we ask over and over again: "Why me, why did this happen to me?" So we come to this synagogue on *Erev Yom Kippur* repentant, but we come with such pain as well.

On the evening of the Day of Atonement, after *Kol Nidre*, Rabbi Levi Yitzchak of Berditchev, "the poor man's rabbi," asked an illiterate tailor, "Since you couldn't read the prayers today, what did you say to God?" "I said to God," replied the tailor, "Dear God, You want me to repent of my sins, but my sins have been so small. I confess, there have been times when I failed to return leftover pieces of cloth to the customers. When I could not help it, I even ate food that was not kosher, but really, is that so terrible? Now take yourself, God, just examine your own sins. You have robbed mothers of their babies and have left helpless babies orphans, so you see that your sins are much more serious than mine."

Our first natural response is to blame God and to be angry at God. How could God let this happen? What kind of a God would do this to me? That anger alienates us from our God and our tradition. Religious acts, prayer, fasting, all become meaningless, because it all seems absurd. If this kind of tragedy can happen, what good is religion, what good is religious faith?

Our second natural response is to turn that anger inward, in our search for someone to blame, in our search for understanding. What did *I* do to deserve this? And we struggle with our own easily exploited feelings of guilt, as we try to make sense of our tragedy. It must be some kind of punishment. *I* am guilty. I did something wrong – and we easily become consumed by accusations of self and by self-hatred.

In one way or another, each of us has been wounded by the tragedies in our lives. How do we keep our wounds from standing between us and God? How do we keep them from standing between us and our better selves? Generations of Jews have felt this kind of pain and suffering and continued to have faith in God, and in themselves. How?

The two reactions I've described, anger at God and anger at self in the form of guilt, stem from a common, but all too simple, perspective on the nature of our universe. They come from the classical idea that God is all-powerful and all-good, all the time. If we accept this principle, then the existence of undeserved evil in our world becomes impossible to explain. If God is all-powerful, God should have kept this horror from occurring. If God did not do so, God must be capricious, or uncaring, or downright evil at times, and clearly untrustworthy.

And if God is truly both powerful and good, then the suffering must somehow be deserved. The only way to maintain God's integrity then is to blame oneself, so that the system works and the evil is just. Those who are affected are being punished for something.

Judaism has never been willing to settle for these very human and understandable, but so deeply unsatisfying and limited, responses to the problem of evil. Each generation has struggled with its own experience, and put forth theories for further consideration, some more satisfying than others.

The conflict brought the rabbis to posit the existence of the *Olam Ha-ba*, the world to come. If we see unjust suffering all around us in the world, they thought, we will surely see it rectified, after our deaths, in some kind of eternal existence, where the good will be justly rewarded and the evil will suffer. There was a measure of hope in this perspective, and some people clung to it. But others refused to be satisfied with an other-worldly solution, when they were not even sure they believed in another world after death. They wanted to push the question farther, to see what could be understood about the existence of suffering in *this* world.

Jewish thought then moves quickly to a notion that is difficult and painful for us, but which must be considered in some measure. It is argued that there is a great deal more evil and suffering in the world caused by humanity than we take responsibility for. For instance, we typically blame God for airplane accidents, but they most likely come from human error or neglect; we blame God for countries of starving people, but there are resources enough to feed everyone were the resources allocated carefully and properly; we blame God for deaths from drunk driving, but we have created a world in which alcoholism is a disease of epidemic proportions.

Jews always have believed that God created humanity with free will, with the capacity to distinguish good from evil, and with the opportunity to do so. Were God to make our choices for us, we would simply be puppets, and would lose our essential humanity. As

Evil and Faith

a species, we were created with the responsibility to choose right over wrong, life over death. And so often, we make the wrong choices. Sometimes knowingly, sometimes not, sometimes out of laziness, sometimes because we cannot quite see the whole picture, less out of an intention to do evil, than out of a lack of understanding of our own power, as individuals, and as a people, to affect the way the universe works. The great Rabbi Maimonides wrote: "Most evils that befall individuals are due to themselves . . . . When we suffer from the evils we have brought upon ourselves by our own free will, we attribute them to God – far be it from Him!"*

I include this thought not to encourage us to feel even more guilty, but to help us minimize our anger at God, and to begin to penetrate the wall that separates us from God. God is not responsible for a tremendous number of the injustices we ascribe to God; humanity is, and we need to consider again the tremendous potential, within us, to create good or evil.

Still, we know that human limitations and failings cannot account for all the suffering in our world. There are tragedies for which we can see no cause and which seem to have no benefit. Theologians have argued that we learn from our pain, that our suffering causes us to grow, and while that seems to be the case, the thought is easily and quickly countered by the question: "Why would God set up such a cruel system? Could it not have been otherwise, could we not learn to grow and mature in some less painful way?" And we are left with the original question: "Why me? Why have these terrible things happened?"

---

*Maimonedes, Moses. *The Guide of the Perplexed*, Abridged with Introduction and Commentary by Julius Guttman. Indianapolis: Hackett Publishing Company, Inc., 1995. Book III, Ch. XII, p. 150.

Leaning on God

The core answer in Jewish life, from the earliest days of our history up to the present moment, is that there is evil in human existence that we simply cannot explain or understand. Currently, it is beyond us. Our knowledge as human beings is actually fairly limited and, although we like to think of ourselves as sophisticated and wise, the workings of the moral universe are well beyond us and we are left with the sad truth that we just do not know.

I believe that, as with the Biblical Job, the human task is to persevere. While we may be unable to understand the reason behind our particular tragedies, and although we cannot see clearly where humanity is headed, our responsibility is to maintain the faith that there *is* ultimate meaning and ultimate purpose to human existence. That is what it means to be a religious person. It is not to have all the answers, nor to prove the existence of God. It is to find courage to believe that there is meaning to it all.

One way to such faith is to consider the possibility that we are living in the very earliest stages of human development. Human beings have been around for some 50,000-75,000 years and we have learned a great many things. But what will we learn during the next 50,000, and during the 50,000 after that? Our task is to keep the human enterprise alive, to learn to the greatest extent that we can and to *know*, that what we do not understand or achieve will be understood and achieved in future generations. Then it is possible, even when we cannot find meaning in our individual suffering, nevertheless to see meaning in the larger span of time. Humanity is growing, leading to a time when more will be understood and meaning will make itself clear.

We live our lives, constantly, on two different levels of being. We live in the microcosm, the level of our own lives, and the lives of those we love. On this level we struggle, we grow, we try to learn from our suffering, and often we do. We try to achieve some sense of contentedness, and sometimes we do. But when we do not, and when our suffering seems only absurd and inexplicable, it is possible to see our lives in the context of the macrocosm, in terms of the future existence of humanity. Then we can *know* that our lives have meaning and purpose, in that we are the connecting link to a time when more will be known, and that it is possible that our sufferings and our tragedies make sense, in the great scheme of things.

This is the vision that can give us the strength and the comfort to return to our lives, and to ask the quintessentially Jewish question. "Did you ever notice," asks Rabbi Pinchas Peli, "that the book of Lamentations, written out of the great mourning caused by the destruction of the First Temple in Jerusalem, in 586 B.C.E., begins not with the word '*Lama*,' 'why,' but with the word '*Eicha*,' 'how'"? The Jewish question is "how"; how will we respond, how will we live our lives now? The "why" may come; it may not. But the "how" we have control over. The "how" is the challenge to us, to continue on our journey, to make what sense of it we can, to make our individual journeys count as much as we can, and then have faith, in the longest run.

The *Baal Shem Tov* said: "All of humanity's sorrow is felt by the *Shechinah*, by God's presence. When a human being is in sorrow, even the *Shechinah* weeps."

God is not divorced from our sorrow and is not the cause of our pain, but is a partner in it, as God is a partner in our joy.

In each prayer service we sing the words "*Ba yom ha hu, yhiyeh adonai echad, u'shmo echad.* On that day God will be one, and God's name will be one."

On *that* day, not on this day. Someday, if we keep going, we, together with God, will create a purely good and purely comprehensible world. But until that day, we must see that, like us, God is in the process of growing. Rabbi Henry Slonimsky teaches: "God and the world of creatures grow together, dependent on one another for progress. Maybe God and perfection are at the end and not at the beginning," *We*, however, are only at the beginning.

A radical notion – God needs us, and our faith, in order to keep growing. God and humanity are struggling together towards creating a perfect world, a world in which tragedy and pain are comprehensible or even done away with, as our ancestors imagined it could be in the world to come.

On this *Erev Yom Kippur*, may we find the courage to see ourselves as partners to God, not as adversaries of God. May we find the strength of Job, to accept our tragedies, to deny our guilt, to continue on our journeys, with the faith that, together with God, we are building the *Ha-ba*, the world to come.

FAITH IN THE UNKNOWN

Tonight, we have read the third *parasha* from the Book of Exodus, which takes us up through Chapter 13, and I want to tell you, this stuff makes great reading. If you are ever inclined to sit down with a Torah text and just read to enjoy its power and passion, these are the chapters to read.

In preparation for speaking tonight, I did just that. I started at the beginning of Exodus and read right through Chapter 13, without commentaries or pauses, and was reminded what first-class storytelling this is. I urge you: take a copy of the Torah commentary home with you if you need to, and just read these chapters; they are some of the easiest and most satisfying religious reading around.

As I reached this *parasha* in my own reading, I was especially moved by remembering precisely where we were as we read these words last year. It was January 16, 1991. Ralph and I had just returned from our honeymoon to the news that the Persian Gulf War had finally begun. That Tuesday night, we all came together in this room in all of our fear and anxiety, to try to make sense together of the mind-boggling events that were unfolding.

I went back and read the words I spoke to you that night. They were based on three verses from this Torah portion. I quoted the Torah speaking about the ninth plague. It said: "A darkness will come upon the land, a darkness that can be touched." And we surely felt that such a darkness had come upon us and our whole world.

Second, we read: "but all the Israelites enjoyed light in their dwellings." I asked: Where does that light come from; what is its source? And answered: it must come from our inner strength, from our inner being. We could not simply tell each other that everything would be all right, with certainty and with honesty, but we could demand of ourselves courage, hope, and optimism, tools with which we could combat the darkness.

The third text came from a part of the story in which Moses insists to Pharaoh that he must take all of the livestock with him, when he and the Israelites go a three-day's distance away to celebrate their festival and bring offerings to God. (This, remember, was Moses' excuse for getting the people out of Egypt at all.) Moses says: "We cannot know with what we are to worship God, until we arrive there." At the time, I interpreted the text for us as meaning that we cannot know how this war will end or what tragic events will occur in its aftermath; we could not know the end of the story, but we could know that, as a people, we would survive and we would be called upon to praise God then. It would be our responsibility to affirm God's abiding presence in whatever way we could, and to charge ourselves with the task of moving forward, with whatever new reality the world presented to us.

Faith in the Unknown

What struck me now, as I re-read these words a year later, is that this is a model for religious belief throughout our lives. It is a perfect description of how we need to express our belief in God, and trust our faith, every day of our uncertain lives. Faith is what you have when you believe in God's presence and power in the world when you cannot possibly know how things are going to turn out. It was hard for us to model our faith on the Israelites' fleeing Egypt, because we know how it turned out. But *they* did not know, and they must have had enormous faith to leave Egypt after 430 years and follow Moses and Aaron into the wilderness.

Last year I said: "We cannot know precisely how this war with Iraq will turn out, what the costs of it will be." Now we know; we pushed ourselves through some more time until we got farther into the story, and had some sense of how it was going to turn out. Remember, Israel then was being bombed. We were seeing pictures of Israeli families wearing gas masks and Israeli babies in oxygen tents. It was hard to have faith, to make that light from within strong enough to sustain us, and to allow us some sense of calm and grace. Here we are a year later. Some of the results have been terrible of course: Saddam Hussein still has power in the world; we know that the devastation inside Iraq and Kuwait was, and is, horrible; but we are here, we are coping, and our having had faith is justified.

There are so many things that are uncertain in our lives – in our political life, in our economic life, most especially in our personal lives. There are so many stories, the ends of which we cannot yet know. There are fears, frustrations and anxieties, some profound, some trivial, but often causing equal discomfort. When will we learn that the source of hope and strength is there for us to tap into, that God can bring us great strength and peace of mind. For this is

Jewish faith in God. This is the tradition that calls us to fill up our silence when we are waiting in anxiety or pain, with reciting Psalms; that calls us to pray with our community; that asks us to see beyond our limited perspective on life and draw strength and hope from this tradition that has lasted so long.

When Moses begged God for a name by which he could identify God when he would try to get the Israelites to trust him and follow him, he said: "When they ask, 'What is this God's name?' what shall I say to them?" God answered *Ehyeh Asher Ehyeh*, a complicated phrase to translate, but most often understood as "I will be what I will be." To have faith in God, then, is to make yourself strong enough to say: What will be will be, and God will still be present. What will be will be, and we will still find the inner strength to create light.

The tradition offers us this faith, that generations – not every individual, but generations – have had; when we are surrounded by fear, anxiety, and pain, there is still enough goodness, hope, and courage to sustain us until we are linked more securely, once again, to the obvious evidence of God's presence in the world. That very faith is an aspect of God's presence.

A year later, the Persian Gulf War is not as present as it was. "*Ehyeh Asher Ehyeh* – what will be will be, and we will continue to create and lean on God's presence.

11
THE WORLD AROUND US

MARKING KRISTALLNACHT

I would like to describe to you three scenes that occurred during this past week. The first happened right here, in our sanctuary on Family Night. This room was filled with people, with warmth and joy and vitality. We had the kindergarten and first grade class come up to this *bima* to mark the beginning of their religious school studies with the consecration. Those little people marched up here and recited the *Shema* together, they received miniature Torahs, and they began to understand that they are an important part of our community. Our fourth graders presented a play based on the Torah portion. We named a beautiful newborn baby girl. I remember walking in and noticing that all the prayer books were gone from their shelves; that empty bookshelf was a heartwarming sight. Last Friday, in this sanctuary, one could feel the aliveness, the vitality, the richness of the Jewish tradition in all its fullness. Last Friday, our sanctuary was a model of the values we are always trying to teach – it was a place of study, of prayer, of optimism, of acceptance, of love. It was the best the world of religion has to offer.

The second scene took place in the Wilshire Boulevard Temple this past Wednesday night. Seventeen members of our congregation joined over a thousand other Jews from all around Los Angeles for a special ceremony to mark the fiftieth anniversary of Kristallnacht. The term Kristallnacht means Night of Broken Glass, and refers to the organized anti-Jewish riots in Germany and Austria on November 9 and 10, 1938. As a child, I had learned that a very bad riot happened, during which angry people stormed through the streets, and smashed all the windows of all the synagogues, and all the Jewish homes, and all the Jewish businesses in Germany. I did not learn as a child that everything that was to happen during the Holocaust was prefigured on Kristallnacht: that synagogues were burned, that Jewish homes were broken into during the middle of the night, that people were beaten and arrested for no reason other than that they had been born Jewish, that 30,000 Jews were sent to concentration camps that night, that the New York Times reported all this in its front page headline exactly fifty years ago today, Friday, November 11, 1938, and that the world stood by and watched, and no one did anything to help.

So we sat there, in the Wilshire Boulevard Temple, and for two and a half hours watched and listened to a program that tried, in a variety of different ways, to make us feel what had happened, that forced us to remember it, and to think about it all. We saw authentic newsreels of Kristallnacht. A lecture was given by Angus MacLean Thuermer, a non-Jewish journalist (and later a CIA official), who was working for the Associated Press in Berlin in 1938, and was an eyewitness to the events of Kristallnacht. For most of us, the most moving part of the evening was a dramatic presentation called "Six Stories," in which six young, vital, fine actors presented the stories of six children, ages 6-15, who lived in Germany and Austria in 1938, and whose lives were irrevocably changed by the events of Kristallnacht. Each had experienced atrocities, each had watched family and friends disappear and be killed, each had barely escaped death himself or herself.

As the first story came to a close, I thought, "How clever of the author, to make the stories so personal, to remind us that the six million were not nameless, faceless figments of our imagination, but real, individual people. And yet," I mentally criticized, "the author has fictionalized too well. The stories create too perfect a cross section of Holocaust experiences, they are contrived too neatly. What good does it do," I wondered, "to make us hear all the painful details all over again, to stir up all the revulsion and pain we feel, when forced to hear the stories again? We know what happened," I thought. "What is the good of going through this again?"

Finally, the first actor's story was completed, and she said: "This is the life story of Ilse. Ilse is here with us tonight." And a woman walked onto the *bima*. She was an older woman, but not so old; dressed in black, she looked dignified and pained. If you had seen her on the street, you would have found nothing special to remark about her. But she had let her story be told, she had made us remember that all this happened a very short time ago, that it is not ancient history, but the very real story of people who are still alive today.

After Ilse came up, the second story concluded, and a man who had the same look about him walked onto the *bima* – an average person, not so old, dignified and brave, a man who made us understand what the word survivor meant. Ultimately, six of them walked onto that *bima*, six brave souls whose stories we had heard, and cried over. They stood there and silently pleaded with us to know what had happened such a short time ago, to teach it to our children, to force ourselves to come to grips with the reality of what had happened, as they had had no choice in the matter. They had to find a way to face the reality of what began in Germany and Austria, on Kristallnacht, and they had to learn to face life, to choose life, having lived through beatings and fear and separations and death and burnings and unspeakable pain.

We applauded them, as we struggled not to cry, then gave in to tears, realizing that their lives are part of our life. Having lived through these events, they have found the courage to choose life. We must, at least, honor them by remembering what happened, and by struggling with it ourselves, no matter how much we want to close our minds, no matter how futile it seems to hear the stories again.

A third scene. A friend calls me and says: "I went to services last night, and I was so frustrated. I was hoping to hear something about the elections, and the Rabbi talked about Kristallnacht." I said: "Don't you think that's a worthwhile thing for the Rabbi to talk about?" "It's too much," she said. "The kids don't need to hear about the Holocaust anymore. My daughter got it in the fifth grade in religious school and now she's getting it again in the seventh grade. The kids hear about death and destruction wherever they go. If it's not the Holocaust, it's nuclear war, or rape victims, or the environment falling apart. The kids need something optimistic, something happy. They don't need any more depressing, painful things."

I thought about that wonderful family service we had here last week. I thought about our kids' experiencing the warmth and joy of the Jewish community coming together to experience all the richness of a tradition that teaches about life. And I thought about those six survivors standing on the *bima*, and the lives they had led. Both are crucial experiences for us and for our children.

Having been born as Jews, we inherit both ends of the spectrum of life – beauty residing in a tradition of values and rituals, standing alongside the painful side of anti-Semitism in our history. When our children learn the reality of recent history, they will also have the good, positive experience of being Jewish as a backdrop for understanding the pain. Protecting our children from the realities of the Holocaust is not the answer. With all the hard things they have to learn, nevertheless they have to learn about the Holocaust too, and learn about it more than once. Each time I read something about the Holocaust, I explore another range of feeling: a deeper understanding, a different question, a better grasp. We will not overwhelm our children with experiences of the Holocaust, as long as we also give them the gift of the other side of the spectrum, and live a rich, educated, Jewish life, that nurtures us and teaches us to choose life over death of the spirit and the body. Our tradition's richness helps us remember: the Holocaust is not a shameful part of *our* history; it is a shameful part of German history, and of the history of civilization.

You see, it is so easy, if we think about it too much, to think that what has happened to Jews over the centuries somehow has to do with us. Why have such horrible things happened to Jews over the ages? Who needs a tradition of having our children called names and being picked on, that causes me to be in a position of having to teach them about death and destruction. There is a certain sense of self-hatred that is possible, sometimes on the surface and sometimes hidden very deep within us. It is that one moment when we ask: What have we done that is so terrible? Why do people hate us? What's wrong with me? Why do I have to bear the burden of the word Jew?

The second we ask that question, we lose the only meaning it is possible to find in all of this. The instant we forget that it was sickness that caused the Holocaust, *their* sickness, and that it is *their* sickness that continues to cause incidents of anti-Semitism, we lose the lesson it is possible to grasp from this pain. There is ignorance and bigotry and causeless hatred in the world; we have been the victim of it and we have, on occasion, felt it welling up within us. But that ignorance and hatred says nothing about its victims; it speaks worlds about the perpetrators. Racism only teaches us about the people who are racist. Anti-Semitism tells us about the ignorance, stupidity and sometimes violent sadism of anti-Semites.

That lesson must be learned against the background of a child who has been taught all the wonderful aspects of Jewish life. Then, that child can be taught that there are such things as prejudice and ignorance and violence in human nature, and if they are not faced, they can lead to horror. Then, that child can be taught that those things can potentially exist in every one of us. And it is our very Judaism that comes to teach us that we are better than that, that we are creations of God. Other people may learn it from other traditions. To some lucky persons it may be consistently self-evident. We learn about being completely human, about controlling the potentially evil and dangerous parts of human beings, from our Judaism. It has always been what sustains us, what teaches us the joy of life and the necessity to face the evil of life and come to terms with it.

We sat in that vast, beautiful synagogue on Wilshire Boulevard and heard about the destruction of synagogue after synagogue, in Leipzig, in Bamberg, in Munich, in Frankfort, in Mannheim, in Cologne – and sitting there, surrounded by so many other Jews, just for a moment, we felt their fear. What if the synagogue doors were locked? What if flames engulfed us, and anyone who somehow escaped was shot?

We were, for a moment, afraid.

My very dear friend had said: "It's enough of the Holocaust; it's too much. It's too much for the children."

No, it is not too much. It is not enough.

The Kristallnacht observance ended with a musical presentation, a cantata with a written script against a musical background. The ending words taught us the meaning we must find in the Holocaust:

> When good King Hezekiah died
> twenty-five hundred years ago,
> and the people of Jerusalem and Judah
> sought to honor his memory,
> *hoshivu yeshivah al kivro,*
> they built a school over his grave.
> They honored him
> with their commitment
> to the future
> and not with homage
> to his past.
> If we stand proud as Jews
> and teach our children
> diligently
> how to stand beside us,
> then, we, and they, will live.

NEWS FROM THE OUTSIDE WORLD
(MARCH 1994)

So much has happened this week that it's hard to keep up with the news, much less make very much sense of it. Thursday's newspaper screamed out four matters of deep concern to all of us. The most shocking, perhaps, was the bombing of the Israeli Embassy in Argentina. Two hundred and twenty pounds of plastic explosives killed at least fourteen people, maybe as many as twenty, and wounded approximately two hundred and fifty-two others. The wife of the Israeli consul was killed, as was the wife of the embassy's first secretary. Five other Israeli diplomats are missing and believed dead. One Argentine worker was killed, as were a Catholic priest who worked in an elementary school across the street, and a doctor, who simply happened to be walking down the street.

News from the Outside World

The bombing will, of course, be avenged. Foreign minister David Levy went before the Israeli Parliament and said, "We've got an open account of bloodshed with those who set off bombs, both near and far." It was Israel's intention, he said, to "close the account."

Among ourselves, we will have many conflicting feelings about all this.

We will feel the anger and hatred that calls for avenging acts. We will also recognize the seemingly endless cycle of violence in the Israeli-Arab world and feel again the sense of resigned sadness as we wish, hope, and pray that there be another way. Mostly, we feel helpless, as we try to understand, and think of new ways to respond. The daily newspaper in Buenos Aires, *El Cronista*, ran a Page One headline proclaiming: "We Are All Jews." Perhaps there is some solace in that, some hint that the world is coming to realize that what happens anywhere in our small world now affects everyone everywhere, and that, to survive, we will have to find a way of moving toward peace.

Less shocking, perhaps only in that it was more expected, is the clear indication that the subject of the loan guarantees is apparently a dead issue, as the New York Times put it, as long as Mr. Bush is President and Yitzchak Shamir is Israel's Prime Minister. President Bush has chosen to make explicit the linkage of the loan guarantees to building settlements in the West Bank and Gaza, and Prime Minister Shamir will neither let the United States make that decision for Israel nor back off from his absolute position that more and bigger settlements are critical for Israel's continued existence.

Among ourselves, we may disagree on the matter of continued settlements, but we are all pained at the current state of relations between the United States and Israel, the two countries we love, and our anxiety about the future grows. And yet, again according to the

New York Times, there were no signs that senior Israeli officials were in a panic about this matter. Israeli economic planners acknowledged that they will begin a tough and painful process of re-arranging government spending priorities without the loan guarantees, but they are turning to the task. They are also still looking for billions of dollars in overseas loans, even though their credit standing will be lowered without the American guarantees. Nevertheless, even those who stand against the building of settlements feel a certain sense of betrayal by the Bush administration, and a foreboding.

The third matter is quite a different kind. It records a much smaller, drier event, but then, one that might provide some hope. On Wednesday the Israeli Parliament voted to approve a change in the country's electoral system that would provide for direct election of the Prime Minister. As far as I can see, the relative merits of this change are debatable. Those who favor the change say that a Prime Minister directly elected, instead of being appointed by the party that receives the most votes in a general election, would be in a much stronger position to negotiate with the Arabs and to impose financial discipline, less restrained by the power of the party. Those opposed to the change say this will result in nothing more than the election becoming a popularity contest, as some would say has happened here in the United States.

I cannot see that the change makes a significant difference either way. What *is* significant, though, is the matter of change itself. There are many important changes that need to be made, in the way the Knesset is elected, that affect the entire manner in which Israel is governed. Take, for instance, the reality that any party that gets as little as one and a half percent of the popular vote qualifies to have a representative in the Knesset. This is, of course, the system that gives such tremendous power to smaller parties that can make a majority coalition in the Knesset, making their positions enormously influential. That there is any change at all in the electoral system is a wonderfully important thing to note. It means that there is hope in this area, and we can consider ourselves reminded, once again, that change is actually possible, no matter how slowly it may seem to go.

Finally, a remarkably good, and I think even exciting piece of news. This very *Shabbat*, the first woman ever to have had a Bat Mitzvah will follow the tradition of having a second such ceremony seventy years later. In 1922, Rabbi Mordecai Kaplan left the Conservative movement to found the branch of Judaism known as Reconstructionism. In that first year of the new movement, Rabbi Kaplan, who, it ought to be noted, had no sons – often a boon for the feminist movement – trained his daughter Judith for her Bat Mitzvah, which took place on March 18, 1922. Because the biblical lifespan was 70 years, when a person reaches 82 or 83, a second coming-of-age ceremony is in order. Tomorrow, Judith Kaplan, now Judith Eisenstein, will stand before her congregation in Queens, New York, and read from the Torah on her second bat mitzvah.

After a week of news like we have just had, this small event carries an important message. We do survive; we *will* survive. It's the message of Purim, it's even one of the messages of the Holocaust, but more simply and beautifully, this message is carried by this 82-year old woman who will once again chant Torah tomorrow morning. When asked her feelings about all this, Mrs. Eisenstein said, "Bat Mitzvah began not just as a statement of feminism, but as a statement of dedication to something larger than oneself."

If we can see our commitment to Judaism as a matter of being dedicated to something larger than ourselves, we will insure the continued survival of this tradition we love, in the face of pain like this week's news, and we will insure our continued sense of meaning and purpose in our own lives. We do this to be a part of something larger than ourselves alone, because the Jewish community's struggle to do what God wants of us is what continues to make us holy. And, even in the face of a week of news like this week's, it makes us hopeful.

A JOURNEY THROUGH FRANCE
(1991)

The description of building the tabernacle in the wilderness that we read from the Torah tonight reminds me how portable we Jews always have had to be. Although the description was elaborate, filled with items of gold and silver, beautiful yarns and precious stones, it is clear that the accoutrements of the quickly-developing Israelite tradition had to be portable. Indeed, from the beginning, we have been a community of wandering Jews.

This year I was particularly aware of the experience of our people wandering in the country of France. I realized that there were a number of images still in my mind from our trip there that I have wanted to share with you. So before the images get too dim, let me tell you what I observed of our people wandering in France.

Leaning on God

The Encyclopedia Judaica's article on France is some 17 pages long. It begins by stating that the earliest evidence of Jews living in that country comes from the year 6. Jews in France were abundant by 465, it continues, and it then presents a brief history up to the present. Reading these pages is like being on a see-saw. Phrases like "favorable atmosphere" are followed by descriptions of years of forced conversions and expulsions. Finally the negative begins to overtake the positive, and you read of multiple blood libels, holding of Jews for ransom, and the first compulsory wearing of a Jewish badge in the year 1215. The experience of Jews in France, as in all European countries, was one of deeply rooted anti-Semitism that could surface any time, interspersed with periods of prosperous calm, in which Jews also prospered, both economically and religiously.

The first clear image in my mind of experiencing my Jewish identity in France came while I was standing in a circular, cobblestone shopping district in the city of Bourges, feeling in awe of the age of the place. History is ever-present, and I felt acutely aware of the generations of people who had walked the streets before I did, probably in search of some dinner, as I was. As we studied signs in an attempt to get oriented, my eye stopped on a sign for a street named in memory of a citizen of that town who had been deported to Auschwitz. I do not remember the person's name; I stood there stunned by the clarity of the fact that, in this very place, the reality of the Holocaust was present. The Holocaust was not far away, something that happened over there; it was not something that happened back then. It happened right here, to these people, in that place where I stood, and apparently, at least some people in the town were determined not to forget the experience and the individual lives that horror claimed from their own town. An awareness of the closeness of the Holocaust never left me after that moment, until we were back on American soil.

Some days later, we were exploring a town on the other side of the country, called Poligny. It was a town of 5,000 inhabitants, only 100 kilometers from Geneva. Wandering around, we came upon a memorial, which by then I no longer was surprised to see in every small town. The memorial read:

The City of Poligny – To the Children Who Died for France 1914-1918 and 1939–1945

I started to read the names and was surprised: Alexander, Metzger, Meyer – all seemed to be Jewish names. "Don't be silly," I said to myself; "they can't be Jewish names – that's just your own stereotyped idea of what names sound Jewish. Perhaps they're German or Eastern European immigrants to France, not necessarily Jewish." But as I walked around the memorial, I found that none of the other names engraved there in stone sounded Jewish to me; in fact, they sounded typically French. I returned to my first view of the memorial and read the entire wall slowly, carefully. It said:

Alexander, Leon 14 years old
Metzger, Pierre 24 years old
Metzger, Jac 20 years old
Metzger, Auguste 25 years old
Metzger, Bertha 57 years old
Metzger, Juliette 71 years old
Meyer, Paulette 34 years old
Arrested in Poligny April 17, 1944;
Deported to Auschwitz May 25, 1944

I understood. Among the war dead were listed the three Jewish families of Poligny. Did anyone try to help them, I wondered? Did they do their best to protect these Jews up until the end? Or did they all turn their backs in the face of a power greater than they? It is doubtful that any of the Alexanders, Metzgers, or Meyers survived Auschwitz; and yet they are so present in the small, remote town of Poligny, where children must ask their parents about these names and parents must have to explain. I have been thinking so much ever since then, of the power of a name, of how it instantly creates the presence or absence of a person – either way, the person cannot be denied, once you know his or her name. France has not dealt with its historical legacy of anti-Semitism; surely we have not faced all of our feelings about the Holocaust – we can't have, it's still too close. But those names are real, those people were real, and the Alexanders, the Metzgers, and the Meyers *have* been memorialized by their town. The names are engraved deeply in that wall, for future generations to grasp and make sense of that which we can barely imagine.

In Paris we found Jewish life alive and well. We set out Shabbat morning to find the *Mouvement Juif Liberal de France* – the only synagogue in France connected to what we know as the Reform movement. It is a synagogue of about 1200 families, which sounds large, but remember, these are the only Reform Jews in the entire country. We were motivated to go there because I had read that a recently-ordained young woman had become the first and only female Rabbi in France. We found Rabbi Pauline Bebe at the synagogue and learned that she had grown up in that community, had been supported by it during her years of study in Israel and England, and had returned to it with a goal of energizing it, directing it more strongly in a liberal direction and doing comprehensive outreach work to the many, many secular Jews of France who are basically unaware that orthodoxy is no longer the only way to express a Jewish religious identity. Her plan is to remain at this synagogue as an assistant Rabbi for some years, until she feels the time is right to begin a second Reform synagogue in France, which she will then attempt to do. I found her to be a very brave person with endless work ahead of her.

We were privileged to be witnesses to a Bat Mitzvah that Shabbat morning. The service was simple and moving. The emotions were similar to what we feel at such a ceremony here – great pride in the young person's achievements; great hope for the continuation of Jewish life. The service, however, was much more traditional than ours, as we would expect from European Reform. I found myself impressed by the importance of the Hebrew language; although here we read prayers in the vernacular for meaning, as they did, it was the Hebrew that was familiar to us, that bonded us as foreigners with them as Jews. Even if the melodies were different, the *Barechu* was the *Barechu*, the *Shema* was the *Shema*, and we were able to follow the Torah reading comfortably. The Hebrew made us feel at home in a foreign country, where we had been complete strangers.

Many of you have heard already that there was another Rabbi on the *bima* who looked familiar to me. After dismissing him in my mind as the generic Eastern European bearded face that always looks familiar, I was introduced to him after the service to find that he was, until two years ago, our neighbor here in Whittier, California. A coincidence yes, but also another reality of being a Jewish traveler; there *are* connections, acquaintances, similar experiences between Jews of every country. We are, in that way, united as a people, in a way that far exceeds nationalities.

Having met up with another American, we were treated that night to a tour of the Marais district, the traditional Parisian Jewish neighborhood, where we dined in a crowd of Jews celebrating *motzi Shabbat*, the end of the Sabbath, on Sephardic delicacies brought to Paris by North African Jewish immigrants. We felt at home in a way that reminded me profoundly that our Jewishness is never separate from who we are no matter where we are. We are all Jewish travelers, taking that identity with us, wherever we go.

France left me troubled by the roots of anti-Semitism and its presence in the modern world, and by the vitality of those who would devote their lives to creating a visible Jewish life and community in the face of such experiences. I was happy to return to the U.S., to leave some of the oppressiveness of history and the past across the ocean, and more determined than ever to maintain a vital Jewish life in our country, where anti-Semitism, though present, seems neither so entrenched nor so institutionalized. Many questions remain to be answered, many theories of anti-Semitism still to be explored. But, as always, our deepest response as Jews is to continue our journey. We must celebrate one more Shabbat, observe one more Passover, until, in fact, those of us who were slaves to Pharaoh in Egypt have done our part in bringing about a reality in which all human beings are safe and free.

PRECIOUS LEGACY

In 1906, Salomon Hugo Lieben, a high school religion teacher, created an organization for the founding and maintenance of a Jewish museum in Prague. His goal was to collect, preserve and display ritual objects, a task that would illustrate the richness of Jewish life and culture. He scoured Prague, then the surrounding rural villages, then urban auction houses, in his search for the most expressive works of Jewish art. In 1926, the collection had grown so large that Mr. Lieben was granted the use of the largest hall in Prague's Jewish quarter to house his treasures.

In 1941, the Nazis established the Institution for the Exploration of the Jewish Question. The purpose of this institution was to confiscate all Jewish religious objects as Jews were being prepared for deportation to the camps and, true to the methodical character of the Nazis, centralize them in one location. That location was Lieben's pride and joy, the Jewish Museum of Prague.

Leaning on God

In 1942, the name was changed to the Central Jewish Museum. It was to be a scientific study of the extinct Jewish people. Its purpose: to show how primitive and barbaric a people the Jews were.

Jewish museum staff who were forced to prepare the exhibit were able to use their work as a vehicle for an act of spiritual resistance. They prominently displayed items about Passover and Purim, that is, items that symbolized freedom and the joy of redemption from slavery, along with Biblical quotes on hope and deliverance. In their hands, the entire exhibit became a celebration of life and hope.

When the first Nazis to see the museum completed their tour, they ordered three changes: that the exhibit on the ritual of circumcision be expanded; that an exhibit on kosher butchering be added; and that all Biblical quotes be translated.

As we know all too well, little was left of the Czechoslovakian Jewish community after the war, but *this* collection of ritual objects, this Precious Legacy, survived. What remained of the Jewish community in Prague had neither the human nor the financial resources to pursue its legacy and in November 1949 a gift was made of the entire collection to the Czech government. The State Jewish Museum was established formally on April 4, 1950. The exhibit which had started out as a song of praise to Jewish life, and had been so perverted during the Holocaust, had been restored to its original purpose.

Several weeks ago, I went with a group of people from our congregation to New Orleans, to view this Precious Legacy exhibit, which had traveled to the United States. Going through that museum was one of the most moving experiences of my religious life.

The exhibit was set up in a series of different rooms, each room dedicated to a particular value in traditional Jewish life. To walk through those rooms is to grasp for a moment an image of what

Precious Legacy

the perfect Jewish community could be like. The exhibit reflects a pre-modern world, in which the Jewish community was still very tightly knit, and largely separated from the secular world. It reflects a time when every aspect of mundane life was made holy through religious ritual. It creates in your mind's eye a healthy, vital, active Jewish community, a people living out its value in everyday life. Just as I know I have a tendency to glorify the past in general, I am certain that the Czechoslovakian Jewish community was in reality no more perfect than any other Jewish community, and I am sure that there were those who were not dedicated to religious communal life. And yet . . . and yet, one walks away from the exhibit *knowing* why Judaism survives, and knowing that the legacy is precious.

The first room is dedicated to the value of communal worship. Judaism says that not only must Jews pray when they are moved to do so by their own private experience, but also Jews must gather together, as a community, three times a day, to share their thoughts, and needs, and concerns, to schmooze a little, to be together as a community, and to pray. This room has Eternal Lights, *yarmulkes* and *tallises*, and is filled with Torah scrolls and Torah ornaments of the richest beauty you can imagine. There are intricate silver Torah crowns and shields and pointers. Most beautiful of all are the incredible tapestries used as curtains inside the ark, richly embroidered in the finest threads and most delicate fabrics.

The sense of community warmth and concern was unmistakable. You could see women spending hour after hour, working together to create these tapestries and, in the meantime, sharing all kinds of talk, sharing themselves. The most moving Torah curtain was inscribed with the fourth commandment: Honor your father and mother, that you may long endure on the land. It was dedicated by five brothers to the memory of their parents, in thankfulness for the goodness and blessings they gave to their sons. Not one thing in that room was shabby or plain; each object was an expression of deep respect and honor by a community for their way of life.

The second room displayed the cycle of Jewish holidays. Beginning with the shofars of *Rosh Hashanah* and continuing with Chanukah menorahs, Seder plates and Shabbat candlesticks, this display made it clear that hardly a month went by when the community did not gather together for a rich observance. There were several special things in this room: a richly embroidered woman's bonnet and apron, for use on Shabbat only; a matzah roller, fashioned like a rolling pin, but with needles, like a porcupine, to pierce the matzah dough with holes, in the traditional way. Can you imagine a community in which a matzah roller was not a rarity, but a necessary item which individuals used year after year? They *knew*, first-hand, that matzah bakes quickly because of those holes, and therefore was prepared fast enough for the Israelites to take it with them during their escape from Egypt. Also in this room was an *Eruv* plate. In traditional Jewish life, one is forbidden to carry things on the Sabbath, except in one's home. To liberalize this law, the rabbis created the concept of the *Eruv*, which means that a whole neighborhood may be considered the extension of a home, if it is surrounded by a tangible border, like a cord, which clearly identifies its borders, and if the people within those borders share one communal dish of food as a symbol of their commonality. The large brass dish with copper inlays on display was a tangible symbol of this community's devotion to one another and to the Sabbath.

The third room was devoted to Jewish life-cycle events. It acknowledged that each major rite of passage in life was marked in a communal

Precious Legacy

way; at birth, Bar Mitzvah, marriage and death, the Jew was not alone. Circumcision instruments, embroidered cloths in which babies were wrapped for the *bris*, which later were used to fasten Torah scrolls together, Bar Mitzvah books, wedding certificates.

Most moving was the symbol of a ritual process which has long since been taken over by professionals. Each European Jewish community had a *Chevra Kadisha*, a burial society. The members of it lovingly prepared the dead for burial. This was considered to be one of the highest acts of charity because, for this act, there can be no thanks. The *Chevra Kadisha* also took over at the home of the mourners, for the week following burial. During that week, they prepared all meals, relieving the mourners of this burden. On display in this room were a set of china and silver, each piece engraved with the initials of the burial society, which were brought to the mourner's home for use during that week, a silent symbol of the community's presence and support.

The fourth room was dedicated to study and *tzedakah*. In it were precious and rare books and more books, paintings of scholars and a model of a typical library. Here, there was also a collection of charity boxes. No community was without one, and they appeared at all communal gatherings. The most impressive was a large wooden box with a hand reaching out from the top of the box, in the attitude of a beggar's hand. But it was not a frail, human hand; it was an *iron* hand, compelling you to give, to fulfill your responsibility to others.

Four rooms, and in them were the richness and beauty of a traditional Jewish way of life, that imparts a sense of the sacred and that regularly reassures its members that they are not alone, but are part of something much larger. What was so overwhelming was the feeling that if we all followed these rituals and traditions in our modern way, we could create the Messianic era. This exhibit was a blueprint for the perfect Jewish world.

But, of course, it was not the perfect Jewish world. It was the end. It was Hitler, and deportation, and concentration camps, and death.

There was a final room in the exhibit. There were only five objects in it, ritual objects made and used in the concentration camp Theresienstadt. There was a *yarmulke* of rough burlap embroidered with the word Theresienstadt and the year 1945; a wooden Chanukah menorah; a roughly fashioned Star of David; an awkward Seder plate of wood stained with ink; and a crude, pottery Kiddush cup. After seeing fancy silver Kiddush cups lined up one after the other, this pottery cup, in this room, was eloquent.

This is our precious legacy – not the silver and gold and crowns and tapestries, but the song of praise for life, a way of life that was so strong and so valuable that it could transcend the camps. Even amid this most horrific of experiences, people cared enough to fashion these crude implements to fulfill the *mitzvot*. The legacy they left us was faith in the Jewish way of life. Fulfilling the commandments meant community, and community meant survival.

On the way home from New Orleans, I had an experience which I believe was deeply connected to the Precious Legacy. The flight was the worst I had ever been on – pouring rain, lightning every thirty seconds, the plane shaking violently. First several people cracked nervous jokes. Then there was absolute silence. Then a baby cried. For the first time in my life, I found myself thinking that this really could be it; people do die in airplane crashes, and it could happen.

I guess because as a rabbi, I've been to more funerals than most people, my imagination took me to that scene of my family and friends gathered together at my own funeral. The phrase I kept hearing over and over in my mind was the refrain to a Livingston Taylor song: "To my friends a thank you song, for being kind to me. To my friends a thank you song, for being kind to me."

What I wanted to tell those people gathered to mourn for me, was that if they ever doubted it, even for a moment, I knew they loved me, that they had made me feel loved and accepted and part of a community all of my life . . . and that was really the best one could expect from life.

I know there is a connection here between my personal concern to know that if *I* died, people realized it was the community that counted and brought spirituality into the world, and the Jews who died in the camps, leaving behind ritual objects to speak to us of their concern for community and the values our tradition teaches. They gave me and our community the richness of the tapestry of their Jewish life; they gave us the lesson of the love for one another.

"To my friends, a thank you song, for being kind to me." In a burlap *yarmulke* or in a pottery Kiddush cup rests the unsung thank you song of these brave ancestors, the quiet faith of our tradition of community. It is, then, finally, this community that sustains us and teaches us to still say *l'chaim* and still to celebrate life. It is a thank you song for life and community. It is this most precious legacy.

JUST AND UNJUST WARS

I have sat, as you have sat, these past few days, in front of the television news and staring at the newspaper, trying to make some sense out of the information that comes from Iraq, Jordan, Kuwait, and Kennebunkport. It is hard to grasp what is actually happening; it is harder to form an opinion about what *ought* to be happening. Do we have good reason to be in the Persian Gulf at all? Over what issues, exactly, are the battle lines being drawn? Do the issues justify the potential loss of life? Will the United States go to war? Will it be a war worth fighting?

I have no answers, only more questions. I turn to the Torah portion for this week and read: "When you take the field against your enemies . . . ." So I face the reality, to begin with, that our tradition historically believes that there is a time for war. We are more familiar with this point of view from the words of Ecclesiastes: "There is a time to love and a time to hate, a time of war and a time of peace."

Just and Unjust Wars

So I look to find out what else the tradition tells us about going to war. I find that there are two kinds of war discussed – obligatory war, called *milchemet mitzvah*, and optional war, *milchemet reshut*. The obligatory war is defined as war to conquer the land of Israel as well as a defensive war fought to assure Israel's survival. Let us, for the moment, take these as universal prescriptions, rather than as a prescription for the Israelite people only. Thus, an obligatory war could be an offensive or defensive one in which we fight to achieve, or maintain, our existence, self-determination or freedom. Any other war is considered optional.

The difference between these two kinds of wars is spelled out in the verses immediately following the ones we read. The text lists the persons who may be exempted from war: the one who has built a house, but not dedicated it; the one who has planted a vineyard but never harvested it; the one who has paid the bride-price for a wife, but not yet married her; and the one who is afraid and disheartened. All of these, we learn, are exempt from war, but only from an optional war. In a *milchemet mitzvah*, an obligatory war, not only must these people join in the battle, but the *Mishnah* even teaches that for a *milchemet mitzvah*, the obligatory war, just as the bridegroom must go from his chamber, so must the bride come from her canopy.

So we ought at least to ask the question. Would a war in the Persian Gulf qualify as an optional war or an obligatory war? Would it help us to secure or preserve basic survival and freedoms or is it about something less critical to our lives? The Torah text points out to us so clearly what is at stake. The ones who have built a new house, or planted a new vineyard, or are about to be married are exempt from the optional war for one common reason: they are not expected to come back, if they go. Those who are at these tender moments in their lives are not asked to forfeit these experiences unless the fight is for survival. The text rubs it in for us: you cannot expect those who go to war to come back.

The most frightening emotion I have experienced related to this crisis, and perhaps you have shared it, is, strangely enough, excitement. There is, without a doubt, an excitement to huddling around television sets, waiting for the latest news; of exchanging these bits of information with others; of feeling more united as a people because we are facing a crisis; even, of going over there and showing these people what they can and cannot do, in the civilized world.

And the Torah asks us to consider the price. Those whom you send to war, you cannot expect to come back.

Let me return to the text again and quote it for you: "When you take the field against your enemies, and see horses and chariots, forces larger than yours, have no fear of them, for the Lord your God is with you. Before you join the battle, the priest shall come before the troops . . . and say to them: 'Let not your courage falter. Do not be in fear or panic or dread of them. For it is the Lord your God who marches with you, to do battle for you against your enemy, to bring you victory.'" It is a very beautiful prayer.

Surely, every people, of every nationality, and every religion, have a similar one. So we come upon the ancient philosophical puzzle: if two soldiers on opposing sides pray equally to the one God, who can count on having the prayer answered?

You expect *me* to answer that question?

What I *will* tell you, is that for us to have faith at such a moment, to believe in God, if you will, it will require that we believe deeply and firmly and completely in the issue for which we are fighting. And that is what we need to have in our minds, first and foremost, as we consider whether we support military action in the Persian Gulf.

Finally, I turn to an editorial in this morning's L.A. Times written by Ramsey Clark, former Attorney General. Now this is a person whose biases are well known. We would *expect* him, as an anti-war figure, to come out on the side demanding the immediate withdrawal of all U.S. forces from the Persian Gulf region, which he does. But I quote his words, not because of the conclusions, but because he points out some serious items for consideration and asks some serious questions. He notes that President Bush has offered no explanation of the source of his power unilaterally to commit American military forces to foreign territory half a world away, and wonders why no one has questioned his constitutional right to do so. He points out the huge human risk here, not only for Americans, but also for millions of Iraqis, Kuwaitis, Saudi Arabians, and foreigners in these countries. He suggests that President Bush's actions have pre-empted the possibility of Arab, regional, or United Nations' efforts to resolve the problems created by Iraq's invasion of Kuwait. And, whether rightly or wrongly, he takes the position that everyone understands that oil is the issue. Had oil not been present, he says, the United States' reaction to Iraq would have echoed Henry Kissinger's reaction to the terrible Iran-Iraq war – let them kill each other.

He further asks: "What will be the economic impact of this crisis for the world economy and our own? How high will oil prices and inflation grow? How many jobs will be lost? How many billions of dollars will we spend in this adventure? How high will taxes go to pay for it, and how many social services programs will be cut? How will poor nations fare after the conflict? How long will the people of the United States, with no voice in determining their destiny, risk the consequences of an Imperial Presidency?"

They are questions we need to answer, before we dare pray the words of our ancestors, to the Lord our God, who will not let our

Leaning on God

courage falter, who will not cause us fear or panic, or dread, who marches with us to do battle for us against our enemies, to bring us victory.

III
OUR EMOTIONAL LIVES

ANGER

I sit in my office and listen to you. I listen over cups of coffee at the *Oneg Shabbat* and over sheets of papers at board meetings. I listen in hallways and in doorways. I listen to my friends and my family and to the passions of my own heart. And what I have learned this year is that we are angry. We are angry in small ways and important ways, over matters trivial and over matters unbearably profound.

In our daily lives, we lose our tempers quickly. We yell at our children and snap at each other in meetings, in our marriages, over the dinner table. How many of the acts we repent for on this *Yom Kippur* evening stem from our uncontrolled anger?

We are grateful to live in a time when we are learning the value of experiencing all our emotions; expressing them can clear the air, and sometimes teach, or change behavior. But how much more often, if we are honest, is our anger more like ego run amok?

Our needs are not fulfilled; we do not get what we want; we are not receiving the honor or attention we desire. We allow our rage to build quickly and explode forcefully, and we have done damage before we know it.

What we *know* is that we are right and they are wrong. The tradition teaches that anger and arrogance are partners. It is that arrogance that is the main impediment to our repentance on this Day of Repentance. We begin to review our acts, as we imagine that the Holy One is reviewing them, and instead of allowing ourselves to feel contrition, we find ourselves defensive and confused. How bad was that act really? Wasn't I justified in doing that? Ask *forgiveness*? *He* should ask forgiveness of me! *Give* forgiveness? Why must I?

Our society emphasizes the healthiness of expressing our anger; our tradition emphasizes the humility of considering that being good is more important than being right. This humility allows us to listen calmly, because the other person is, like us, a creation of God. This humility has nothing to do with feeling inferior, but everything to do with nurturing an awareness of one's own limitations in comparison to the vastness of the Creator's creation. Our tradition forces us to ask the essential question: What is our purpose in this existence, in this relationship? Is it to control others to serve our own needs, to hold on to our bitterness over the ways in which we were wronged, to justify and justify and justify our actions and feelings in a way that eclipses the other?

Our tradition begs us to consider the answers filled with humility: We exist to learn and grow, to serve God by honoring others, by building connections, and by making peace.

To serve God – ah, there's the rub. Because even if we are convinced that we can train ourselves to move through many of the petty angers of daily life in ways that are more controlled and more holy, we are left this night with the stark reality of a different kind of anger: the profoundness of our anger not just at others, but at God. It comes to us all, through our experiences of life. So many prayers go unanswered, so many pleas are left unheard. So much suffering is met by God with silence.

I have listened to you this year, and I know: the pain is wrenching, as we stand by our parents, spouses, siblings and children who are struggling with illness. They suffer from Alzheimer's or cancer, they are unable to take care of themselves, their dignity ebbs as mental capacities diminish or as pain and anxiety limit lives that once were rich. We watch in agony and can do little if anything. Why, God? Why allow such misery?

I have listened, and I know: the economic realities are not what we thought they would be. So many of us assumed we could make a good living – and in greater and greater numbers, we cannot. Others of us can, but somehow, lately the rules have changed. Commitments we made, lifestyles we counted on, all are tenuous. We are downsizing. We are scared. We are disappointed and we are angry.

I have listened, and I know: the meaning we thought we would find in our work, in our relationships, is missing. For some the work is endlessly tedious or demeaning. For some it is all-consuming, but purposeless. Some can convince themselves their work is valuable, and nevertheless they are plagued with questions. In the long run, am I doing any good?

Our anger at daily events and our profound anger at God are linked by our desire to have some control over what happens in our lives, and by our conviction that we ought to get what we deserve. But the tradition teaches us over and over again that we have control over nothing but our own character. We have no control over what happens to us, only over the way we react.

The model here is Rabbi Akiva. The legend goes that he set out one night, taking with him a rooster, a lamp, and a donkey. At nightfall, he arrived at a village, and asked for hospitality. The people drove him away with curses and blows. Tired and sad, Akiva made his way into the forest and found a place to settle for the night. As he lay on the hard ground he thought, "And yet, there must be a meaning to this." So he settled himself down to sleep and just as he was dozing, the squawking of his rooster awoke him – and he saw that a fox had carried his rooster away. Realizing that he now had barely enough food to last him his journey, he opened his mouth to curse, closed it again, and said, "In this too, there must be a purpose." Now, unable to fall back asleep, he settles down to read by the light of his lamp and no sooner does he open the book than a gust of wind blows the lamp completely out. Akiva is ready to scream with frustration – he opens his mouth, closes it again and, exercising great control, settles down to sleep, muttering, "From this too, some good must come." Akiva awakes in the morning to find that during the night, his donkey wandered off and was not to be found. Akiva sighs, realizing he must continue his long journey on foot. He reaches down to the depth of his being for strength, and forces himself to say: "Somehow, God, this too, you mean for the good."

So Akiva completes his journey and on the way home, walks through the village where he was so rudely refused hospitality to find that every one of the inhabitants had been killed. Robbers had entered the town, asked for hospitality and been refused. They murdered the whole town. Akiva concludes: if he had stayed in the town, he too, would have been dead; if the robbers had seen his light, or heard his

Anger

animals, they surely would have found him, and killed him. Each of the events that had so frustrated him in fact had kept him moving forward on his journey.

We sit here this *Erev Yom Kippur*, believers and non-believers, almost-believers and sometime-believers; "convince-me-and-I-will-believe" believers and "I-was-a-believer-until-such-and-such-happened" believers. We sit here, wanting to be believers, and I tell you that what our tradition teaches is that belief is a choice. It is a matter of control, just the way learning to control one's daily anger is. It is choosing to say "I will search for value and purpose in each event that befalls me, in order to fill life with meaning." Choosing to find meaning in the seemingly arbitrary and often painful events of daily life does not make things better, and does not explain or justify our losses and disappointments. But it allows us to adjust our perspective so that the pain can be borne, in a life of faith. This, too, has meaning.

You see, it turns out that the amount of suffering in our lives has little to do with the extent to which we are people of faith. There are those whose bitterness and cynicism poisons their lives, at the slightest pain, and there are those who endure more than can be believed with grace and courage.

My personal hero has always been Rabbi Leo Baeck. Leo Baeck was born in Poland in 1873, the son of a Rabbi, and in 1912 became the first Reform rabbi in Berlin. Baeck taught and wrote and preached in that city throughout Hitler's rise to power, and he chose to devote himself to defending the rights of Jews under the Nazis although he had many opportunities to leave. Baeck refused all invitations to serve as Rabbi or professor abroad, declaring that he would remain with the last *minyan* of Jews in Germany as long as possible. Leo Baeck was sent to Theresienstadt in 1943 and there this gentle, courageous scholar continued to teach, console, and speak of the essential dignity of the human spirit, even in the face of all the horrors he witnessed.

Leo Baeck miraculously survived and came to the United States after the war. With all he had seen, with all he had suffered, Leo Baeck lived his life essentially unchanged, faith undiminished. He taught at the rabbinic school in Cincinnati, and preached at a synagogue there. They say that when Baeck lifted his hands to bless the people with the words of the *Y'varechecha* – "May the light of God's presence shine upon you and be good to you" – the congregation felt very close to the Divine Presence. These words, spoken by this survivor, instruct us; the encounter with God can take place in the utmost darkness, if we choose it. Leo Baeck – teacher of Theresienstadt, man of faith. If *he* could choose faith, how dare *we* not?

We control our anger, at one another and at God, by focusing instead on our own humility, by deepening it and enlarging it. There is more going on in the universe than we are privy to. Our task as we move through the angers and frustrations, and the richness and joy of human life, is to remember that we are not God, but we are on a journey towards God. When we choose to focus our lives on that passion, we slowly begin to see the Godly in those with whom we struggle; we renew our strength to struggle against all that is not Godly, to live with faith, in a world in which faith is dismissed as childish, foolish.

Faith was not foolish for Leo Baeck. Nor for Levi Yitzchak, Chassidic rabbi of Berditchev, known far and wide for his anger at God and his willingness to call God to task for all the world's sorrow. They say that one year, as *Kol Nidre* was about to begin, Levi Yitzchak stood before the ark as the sun was setting. For a long time he stood there,

Anger

silent, still. The sun was down and his disciples became alarmed; it was time to begin the holiest prayers of the holiest day of the year, and their rabbi, Levi Yitzchak, still stood, in silence. In the dark, they debated what to do when, finally, Levi Yitzchak spoke:

"Dear God," he said, "We come before You this year, as we do every year, to ask Your forgiveness. But in this past year, I have caused no death, I have brought no plagues upon the world, no earthquakes, no floods. I have made no women widows, no children orphans. God, you have done those things, not me. Perhaps you should be asking forgiveness from me."

The great Rabbi paused, and continued in a softer voice. "But, since You are God, and I am only Levi Yitzchak: *Barechu et Adonai ha-Mevorach*," "Praised be the One to whom our praise is due." And he began the service.

Anger is not an end in and of itself. It is something to be moved through and learned from, as we search for, and choose, a life of faith.

Oh God, my God . . . open my heart and the hearts of all your people Israel to a *Shalom Rav*, a great peace, a peace that comes in spite of pain, in the face of our anger, the peace that focuses us on our journey toward You and Your truth. Help us know that without You, there is no meaning, that in choosing You, we ennoble ourselves and our world, and create the only possibility for meaning and joy.

RECONCILIATION

Jacob and Esau, two brothers deeply connected to each other, nevertheless endure twenty years of silence between them. They have justifiable reasons for their anger and resentment. They were two completely different young men who valued different things. Their parents took sides; the father Isaac took Esau's side against his wife Rebecca, who took Jacob's side, and this had to push the two brothers apart even further. Jacob had done terrible things. He had bribed Esau's birthright away from him at a moment when Esau was weak and could easily be exploited. And Jacob stole Esau's blessing, his inheritance, by tricking their father Isaac into giving Jacob the blessing when he believed he was giving it to Esau. Jacob had good reason to fear his brother Esau's anger even after all these years had passed. He had inflicted enormous pain.

And yet, the time had come, as it has to come eventually in almost any damaged human relationship, for some healing to occur. Jacob knew that even with all the pain and all the time gone by, there were things that tied him to his brother, bonds that had not eroded, and that could be saved. So Jacob sends messengers to Esau: "Come talk to me." And Esau agrees to come.

Then Jacob panics. Jacob is terrified about what Esau might do or say. So he starts making a very complicated set of arrangements for the meeting. He divides his people and his flocks into two separate camps, in case it is revenge Esau seeks.

If one camp is attacked, the other at least would be safe. He selects and prepares tremendous gifts for Esau – goats and rams and camels. He sends messages full of humility, messages signed: "Your servant, Jacob." And he prays.

You can feel Jacob's fear as he anticipates Esau's arrival. You *know* the torture he is putting himself through: "How will he react? What will he say? What will *I* say? Will he give me a chance to say *anything*?"

Finally, Jacob sees Esau coming, and Jacob moves toward him, bowing low to the ground seven times. You can see him, slowly rising up the last time, to meet Esau's eyes, terrified that he would see only rejection there. So Genesis, chapter 37, verse 4 says "Esau *ran* to greet him. He embraced him and, falling on his neck, he kissed him, and they wept." After all Jacob's pain, after all his anticipation and fear, Esau *runs* to meet him.

Most things are worse in anticipation than in actuality. It is our own fears and insecurities and doubts that are so harsh – much harsher, usually, than the reality of whatever it is we need to face. Esau *ran* to Jacob, and reached out for him.

The reason Jacob is a hero is that he did not let all his anticipatory fear stop him. He did not become immobilized. He took what could have been a completely overwhelming experience and found ways to keep going. He busied himself in particular tasks. He did not ask himself "What will happen if all this fails?" Instead, he just kept doing things, one after the other: He sent the message to Esau, he took what precautions he could by separating into two camps, he prepared gifts, and he prayed. At any moment, all that anticipation, all the possible rejection and anger, could have frozen him in his tracks – but it did not. "And Esau ran to him."

On top of it all, Jacob did not ask for certainty. He did not wait until he could say for sure that Esau would react favorably to him. He was wise enough to know that such a moment never comes. For most of us, most times, there is no way to know how it will come out. To wait for certainty is to become immobilized. Jacob lived through all the horrible anticipation, yet did not become immobilized. He faced the fact that there was no way to know whether he would be successful or not.

Some months ago, a dear friend of mine turned forty years old. For two months before the birthday, she was obsessed and panicky and could talk about nothing but what it meant to turn forty. On the birthday itself, I remarked to her that she seemed so calm and not at all upset that the big forty had finally arrived. She shared with me then, this section from *Through the Looking-Glass*:

> Alice was just beginning to say "There's a mistake somewhere –," when the Queen began screaming, so loud that she had to leave the sentence unfinished, "Oh, oh, oh!" shouted the Queen, shaking her hand about as if she wanted to shake it off. "My finger's bleeding! Oh, oh, oh, oh!"
>
> Her screams were so exactly like the whistle of a steam-engine, that Alice had to hold both her hands over her ears.

Reconciliation

"What *is* the matter?" she said, as soon as there was a chance of making herself heard. "Have you pricked your finger?"

"I haven't pricked it *yet*," the Queen said, "but I soon shall – oh, oh, oh!"

"When do you expect to do it?" Alice asked, feeling very much inclined to laugh.

"When I fasten my shawl again," the poor Queen groaned out: "the brooch will come undone directly. Oh, oh!" As she said the words the brooch flew open, and the Queen clutched wildly at it, and tried to clasp it again.

"Take care!" cried Alice. "You're holding it all crooked!" And she caught at the brooch; but it was too late: the pin had slipped, and the Queen had pricked her finger.

"That accounts for the bleeding, you see," she said to Alice with a smile. "Now you understand the way things happen here."

"But why don't you scream now?" Alice asked, holding her hands ready to put over her ears again.

"Why, I've done all the screaming already," said the Queen. "What would be the good of having it all over again?"*

Usually, the anticipation is much worse than the actuality. And the trick is to just get through it, even if you have to scream your way through it, as the Queen did. You just get through it, and then it is gone.

Two other lines of dialogue between Jacob and Esau help us understand the enormity of their reconciliation. After they had talked for a few moments, Jacob says to Esau: "To see your face is like seeing

---

* Carroll, Lewis. *Alice's Adventures in Wonderland* & *Through the Looking-Glass*. New York: New American Library, 1960. P. 173.

the face of God." For him to have been courageous enough to face Esau, after all that had happened, was a way of acknowledging God's presence in this world. When people get through the fears involved in doing what they know is right, that is a way of seeing God's presence.

Finally, Esau says to Jacob, "Let us start on our journey, and I will proceed at your pace." When Jacob found the courage to take the first step, all of a sudden, there was support, someone to say: "O.K. I'll slow down, I'll do it your way, I'll try to acknowledge the risk you took and how hard it was for you – I want to help – let us walk at your pace."

We all have our Esau. We all have someone or something we are spending so much time and energy anticipating that we have become immobilized. Perhaps it is a job change or a move. Perhaps it is a mother, or brother, or friend to talk to about something that could cause real conflict. Perhaps it is a letter you need to write to someone with whom you have unfinished business,

If we behave like Jacob and refuse to become immobilized by our own fears, then at least we have a chance of getting a reaction like Esau's: Esau ran to Jacob and he walked together with Jacob at Jacob's pace.

HOPE

So there I was, living in Jerusalem, during my first year of Rabbinic school. Every day I would dutifully struggle to read one of the Hebrew newspapers, but eventually I would give up and turn to the Jerusalem Post, the condensed, but English paper, intended for newcomers. There I would get my reward: *Dry Bones*. For those of you who do not know, *Dry Bones* is a daily Israeli comic strip. It is also the funniest political and social satire around, sort of an Israeli *Doonesbury*. Reading *Dry Bones* was something we looked forward to every day.

Now you might ask: what kind of a name is *Dry Bones* for a comic strip? I certainly did; I wondered about it all the time. Let's see – dry must refer to dry humor; bones must be related to the expression "No bones about it." I could not figure it out, and eventually got so used to it I did not even wonder about it.

Leaning on God

Not until the end of the year, when I was leaving Israel, did I solve the mystery. I bought several books that were collections of *Dry Bones* cartoons and inside the cover of each I found printed the words of the prophet Ezekiel that we read this morning:

> The hand of the Lord came upon me. He took me out by the spirit of the Lord and set me down in the valley. It was full of bones. He led me all around them; there were very many of them spread over the valley, and they were very dry. He said to me, "O mortal, can these bones live again?" I replied, "O Lord God, only you know." And he said to me, "Prophesy over these bones and say to them: 'O dry bones, hear the word of the Lord. I the Lord will cause breath to enter you, and you shall live again. And you shall know that I am the Lord.'"
>
> He said to me: "These bones are the whole House of Israel. They say: 'Our bones are dried up, our hope is gone, we are doomed.' Therefore say to them, thus said the Lord God: 'I am going to open your graves, O my people. I will put my breath into you and you shall live again.'"

Dry Bones – a symbol of renewed change, growth – a symbol of hope. Ezekiel's crazed, almost psychedelic vision of a valley filled with bones coming alive again, those bones being rebuilt into a living, breathing people, struck me with a force that I have infrequently felt before or since from any Biblical text.

Those bones represented the refusal to accept even total devastation without some hope. If the dry bones could live again, then the Jewish people could reclaim the land of Israel. If the dry bones could live again, then secular and assimilated world Jewry could find a new sense of spirituality, and our Jewish tradition could be a vital part of

Hope

our lives again. If the dry bones could live again, then each of us can face the trauma and devastation that happens in all of our lives, with the knowledge that nevertheless there is purpose and there is meaning.

These dry bones mean that there is hope, and what *might* be a haunting, frightening image – the rattling of the bones rising up out of the valley and forming themselves into skeletons, and eventually coming alive – this image becomes instead a vision of hope. Ezekiel's vision of Dry Bones reminds us that *we can, we can*, whatever the task.

For several days now, I have been puzzling over why this passage is read on the Sabbath during Passover. In many cases, the answer to such questions can be found in the connection between the Torah and the Haftorah portions. The Torah portion read this morning describes the giving of the second set of tablets on which the Ten Commandments are engraved. The first, Moses has smashed in fury over the worshipping of the golden calf, but God is pictured not as being angry, like Moses, but as long-suffering. God says to Moses, "Carve two tablets just like the first and I will inscribe them, just as the first."

By all rights, God should have been ready to give up on the Israelite people. They had done nothing but complain since leaving Egypt, and even had argued that they would have been better off enslaved there than free in the desert. They questioned Moses' authority and finally rebelled completely, losing faith in God and dancing around the golden calf. Faced with utter defeatism, God responds with hope: "Carve a second set of tablets." They will learn. They will change. There is hope.

This is the tie between the Torah and Haftorah portions. With no reason to hope, God believes in the Israelite people. With no reason to believe, Ezekiel believes that the Valley of Dry Bones will be rejuvenated, that the people of Israel can live again.

Leaning on God

On Passover, against all reason we express our belief that the Messianic era is achievable. We eagerly await Elijah's entrance, and we swear that we saw the wine in Elijah's cup diminish just a little bit – so strongly do we want to believe in the future. We close our Seder with the joyous toast – "Next year in Jerusalem," meaning "Next year may all people be free."

Passover is almost always called the holiday of freedom. But lately I have begun to think of it more as a holiday of hope. Freedom surely was a gift from God as we escaped from Egypt and, as a result, we know that all human beings desire that same freedom. But hope, hope is a value that winds its way throughout the Passover story. It is not a one-time gift. It is, instead, the knowledge that if we solve one problem after another, as they arise, we are doing all we can to bring about the Messianic era and to lead good, productive, satisfying lives.

When all the sons of Israel were being killed in Egypt, Moses' mother and sister refused to accept defeat and floated the baby Moses down the Nile in the mere hope that someone would find him.

Moses, after years of exile from Egypt, terrified of returning there to face Pharaoh and to face his own identity, unconvinced that he, of all people, could argue with Pharaoh, resolutely gathers his strength and takes those first steps toward Egypt with only the hope that he will know what to do next.

Reaching the shore of the Red Sea, with Pharaoh's army directly behind, Moses refuses to surrender his hope, and marches towards the water, knowing that something would happen, hoping, that if he had the courage to keep going, the rest somehow would take care of itself.

God, Moses, Ezekiel, you and I – all we need is the vision of perfection in front of us and the courage to hope.

Hope

These dry bones can live: the dry bones of own lives; the dry bones of our relationships; the dry bones of our Jewish heritage; the dry bones of our Messianic hope for the world. We can breathe the very breath of life into the dry bones, if we are not afraid to take that one small step, to do the one thing we *can* do.

On this Festival of *Matzot*, inspire us to goodness. On this Day of Liberation, make us a blessing. Make us worthy of the Messianic promise of a world that is yet to be.

How many images this moment brings to mind, how many thoughts the memory of Elijah stirs in us – the times when we were objects of distrust, when our doors were open to surveillance, when ignorant and hostile men faced our doors with terror. We will not die, but live, live to declare the works of God. And we will praise *Adonai* forever.

Each drop of wine we pour is hope and prayer: that people will cast out the plagues that threaten everyone, everywhere they are found, beginning in our own hearts. Each drop of wine reminds us that God can re-invigorate these dry bones.

PERSONAL PRAYER

It is always a bit unnerving to begin reading the book of Leviticus from the Torah. After the magnificent heights of the book of Exodus – the departure from Egypt, the parting of the Red Sea, and the giving of the Ten Commandments – the excruciatingly detailed bloody descriptions of the animal sacrifices our ancestors brought before God are troubling and distasteful. Our annual introduction to the world of sacrificial offerings often motivates me to create sermons on widely divergent topics, as we collude together in ignoring this facet of our tradition.

This year, instead of being turned off by the descriptions of the sacrifices, I feel drawn to them. Surely, the sacrifices were awesome and powerful in their time. Perhaps there is still something of value that studying them can give us.

Bringing sacrifices to gods was virtually universal among the ancients. People of varied belief systems brought food and drink, perfumes, incense, grain, fruit and wine as offerings. The most common and, at the same time, surely the most intense of the sacrifices, was the burnt offering of an entire animal, the *olah*, the description of which we read from the scroll tonight.

In the world of ancient Israel, these offerings were made to God for four different reasons. Sacrifices were made either in the hope of getting something, in the attempt to ward off a disaster (that is, the hope of *not* getting something), in the effort to achieve purification from sin (by the way, this only worked for unintentional sin), or in the expression of a sense of reverence and thanksgiving. Each of these desires relates to a single concern: to bring an individual closer to God.

You can see this perhaps most clearly in the case of unintentional sin. The individual inadvertently has hurt another person. The unintentional sinner experiences a sense of guilt, feels pain for the other, and carries an internal sense of uncleanliness. The individual now has a deeply-felt need somehow to experience God's presence, and once again to draw nearer to and feel accepted by God. So the person brought a sacrifice, a *korban* in Hebrew. This word *korban* itself gives us one of the main clues. It literally means to draw near. On the surface, it appears to have been used to describe the manner in which a person drew near to the altar in order to sacrifice the animal. But it is striking that the same word expresses this need to draw oneself near to God's presence and, even more powerfully, to draw God near, to pull God close to you.

Until the Romans burned the Temple in Jerusalem in the year 70 C.E., this *korban*, the sacrifice, as gory as it might seem to us, was the Israelites' method for pulling God close. After this time, we know, of course, that synagogues developed all over the world, and that prayer came to take the place of these sacrifices. The desire to

Leaning on God

draw God close and to have some kind of spiritual life in the midst of this all-too-crazy life we live seems to be stronger than ever these days. It is the need I hear articulated most often by many people. "I feel like I am a spiritual person," they might say, "but I don't know what to do about it."

Our ancestors were on to something here. They knew that they needed to draw close to God, and they grew to understand that they could do it with this remarkable gift given to human beings – with words, with speech, with prayer. Many people are skeptical about this when I present it as a path towards a deeper spirituality. They wonder whether they can learn how to pray by themselves, for themselves. They are convinced that they do not know how, that they would feel embarrassed and ill-prepared for an act of personal prayer.

Yet I become more and more convinced that our need to draw close to God will move us to build a system of communication, through personal prayer. It is easier than you think. There are two main steps. The first is to make a time for prayer in your day, preferably at the same time each day, maybe even twice a day. When you get up in the morning, or when you go to sleep at night, when you are alone in your car, or when you are hiding behind the newspaper but not really reading. It does not need to be a long time, especially at first. Second, pick a prayer that you love – the *Shema*, the *V'ahaftah*, the *Motzi*, or a psalm – something you know well and are comfortable with in English or Hebrew. Take a moment to prepare, to focus inward, to sense the best that is in you. Direct it to God, and say your prayer. That's all – something very simple – but the beginning of a pattern that might draw you near, that might help build a relationship to the divine. It is a far cry from animal sacrifice – but then again, maybe not so far at all.

Personal Prayer

When we think of creating personal prayer as a part of our everyday lives, it often seems like a daunting task. We have visions of reading entire services out of the prayerbook, of trying to do at home something similar to what we do here in the sanctuary. Personal prayer could grow into these larger proportions. There are entire services you could pray at home, and you may find you want to do that at some point. But for now, this minute or two of focus, of spoken words, of prayer, will perhaps be enough to express the spiritual dimension of our lives; to help us feel drawn closer, to wrap God's presence around us, like a coat against the cold.

DOUBT

With all my heart I love this week's Torah portion. As a human being, as a Jew, and as a Rabbi, I am obsessed with the question of what it means for a person to have faith in God today. And so we come to the story of the Golden Calf.

Even people who do not know much about the Bible know about the Golden Calf, the quintessential symbol of idol worship. The Israelites had reverted to their old, pagan ways and had given up on the one God who had led them out of Egypt. Today, when we talk about idolatry, we talk about worshipping money or status or our children. According to most sermons, these have become our present-day golden calves, which we worship instead of God.

As I re-read this familiar story this week, I was surprised to find a completely different perspective on it, one that opens up the whole question of what it means to believe in God. I do not believe the

Doubt

Israelites had, in fact, reverted to their pagan ways. Here is the clue: The Torah says that the people asked Aaron to make a God for them and when he produced the Golden Calf, they proclaimed: "This is your God, O Israel, who brought you out of the land of Egypt." The people had not turned to any other God. They were not worshipping a sun God or a moon God; they were still worshipping the one God of Israel who had brought them out of Egypt. They simply wanted proof – visible, verifiable proof – that the one God really did exist.

We make exactly the same mistake today. We keep asking for the proof. "Tell me why I should believe in God." "Give me some evidence that God created the world." "Prove to me that God exists." And that's how we build our golden calf. The crime of the golden calf was not idol worship, so much as it was the need of our ancestors to have concrete proof that the one God who allowed for them to be free from Egyptian bondage really existed. God's presence had been made known to them in the most dramatic way possible. They had been *slaves*; now they were free. Yet, they were unable to affirm their faith in an intangible power greater than they. They needed a physical sign in their midst, a golden calf.

When we ask for verifiable proof that God exists before we are able to assert our religious identities, we worship the golden calf just as surely as our ancestors did. The lesson to be learned is that it is not within the realm of human experience to know God directly, but that the evidence of God's presence is all around us, just as it was for our ancestors. When we see God's presence embodied in what human beings, at their best, are able to do, we move beyond the mistake the Israelites made and become truly religious people.

Moses is probably the ultimate image of the religious person, the only prophet with whom God spoke face to face. Now, why should we honor Moses so? How difficult is it to believe in God through thick and thin, if God is there talking to you? If God were talking directly to me, I would have unshakable faith too. But as I continue to study the legend of the golden calf, I no longer am convinced that Moses knew anything more than we know. God's speaking face to face with Moses is a metaphor, just as surely as our speaking about God as a King is a metaphor. To say that God spoke with Moses face to face is to say that Moses was so sure of his faith that it was *as if* he had spoken with God face to face. If Moses was able to do all the things he did, with no more cold, hard facts about the existence of God than we have, then he is indeed to be idealized as the ultimate religious person.

Look at what happens in the rest of the legend. Listen to the dialogue first, just as it is written in the Torah:

> The Lord spoke to Moses. "Hurry down, for your people, whom you brought out of the land of Egypt, have sinned. . . . They have made themselves a golden calf and bowed low to it. . . ." The Lord said further to Moses: "I see that this is a stiff-necked people. Now, let Me be that My anger may blaze forth against them and that I may destroy them, and make of you a great nation." [Notice, *Moses* is not to be destroyed]. But Moses implored the Lord his God saying: "Let not your anger blaze forth against Your people . . . Turn from Your blazing anger, and renounce your plan to punish Your people. Remember Your servants, Abraham, Isaac, and Jacob, how You swore to them by Yourself and said to them: 'I will make your offspring as numerous as the stars of heaven and I will give to your offspring this whole land of which I spoke, to possess

forever.'" And the Lord renounced the punishment He had planned to bring upon His people.

Now, what if we interpret this conversation as occurring, not between Moses and God, but between Moses and himself, as Moses struggles with his own faith. Imagine that the anger is not God's, but that of a great leader whose people are unable to grasp how wise he is and are unable to follow him. Imagine that it is Moses, not God, saying, "Why do I need these people? I can be a great nation without them." Then Moses, instead of pacifying God, is trying to talk himself into maintaining his faith when all the rest of Israel had lost it. Then Moses is finding the courage to say: "I will not give up on these people, even though they have behaved horribly, and I will not go on my way, but I will affirm my faith in the face of this tragedy and I will use my life to change the way the world is."

Does Moses talk God out of destroying the Israelites? Or does he choose to affirm that there is a God in the universe by not giving up on his ideas? At a time when, I suspect, most of us would have given up any kind of faith in God or belief in a better world, Moses chose to return to the Israelites with the Ten Commandments without any direct command from God.

But things do not get any better; they get worse. Affirming his faith, Moses returns to the Israelite camp and the first thing that happens is that Joshua lies to him. Joshua meets Moses at the foot of the mountain and tells him that the sounds coming from the camp are only the sounds of the people preparing for war, nothing more. But Moses knows better, and he answers: "It is not the sound of the tune of triumph I hear nor the sound of the tune of defeat. It is the sound of song I hear." When Moses comes near the camp and actually sees the Israelites dancing around the golden calf, his anger and his horror overwhelm him. Joshua's lie becomes the symbol for the state the world is in. There is no reason to affirm faith in God, in goodness, in purpose, in anything; there is only dismay and sadness. Moses throws the tablets of Ten Commandments to the ground and smashes them to bits. The perfect man of God has lost his faith. He looks out on the way the world is and cannot find enough reason to believe in God, to affirm that there is purpose to this world.

As we often are, Moses is unable to go on in any positive way. When this happens to us, we say we do not believe in God. And so we give up on purpose and goodness and meaning, and just try to get through our own lives with some comfort.

Moses goes through a long and difficult process before he is able to restore his faith. He argues with Aaron and blames him. He pits the Israelites against one another, allowing those who wish to repent to punish the others with death. And finally, God says to Moses: "Set out from here, you and the people you have brought out of the land of Egypt, to the land which I swore to Abraham, Isaac and Jacob. But I will not go in your midst, since you are a stiff-necked people, lest I destroy you on the way."

Does God remove the divine presence from the people? Or does Moses refuse to acknowledge God's presence all around him because of his own anger? Are we unable to see God's presence because of our own anger and our own doubts? The message from God is this: I cannot be in your midst when you are a stiff-necked people, that is, when you sin. When you do not create me, I am not among you. My presence is dependent on your actions. It is within the human potential to bring about God's presence. When we choose not to, we end up destroying ourselves on the way, as God threatens to do to the Israelites.

Doubt

Once God announced that the divine presence will not be with the people, Moses and God began a series of negotiations or, to put it another way, Moses begins a struggle with himself. Moses is trying to rebuild his faith in God so that he can once again lead the people. He needs to reaffirm his belief in the positive forces in the universe, before he can continue.

The Torah describes how he does this. A Tent of Meeting was pitched outside the camp where it was believed possible to sense God's presence. When Moses entered the tent, a pillar of cloud would descend on the entrance of the tent and Moses would talk to God. How might we interpret this? Moses goes away to a special, holy place where he is absolutely alone, where he attempts to encounter God. And when he does encounter God, it is within a cloud, in a fog – perhaps, in his own confusion.

And what does the Torah tell us of the conversation between God and Moses? Moses says: "You say to me, 'Lead this people forward,' but you have not made known to me whom you will send with me. Further, you tell me I have gained your favor. . . . If I have truly gained your favor, let me know your ways . . . ." And God responds: "I will go in the lead and will lighten your burden."

Moses is struggling to affirm the faith. He *knows* that if he looks for positive value in the world and works to create goodness, his burden will be lightened and he will have created God's presence. God will be with him. But then his doubting side speaks up again. Moses responds: "Unless you go in the lead, do not make us leave this place." God says, "I will do what you have asked." Moses, you see, is letting God back in. But he doubts a third time and asks: "Well then, let me behold your presence God, let me *see* you." God answers: "You cannot see my face but I will make my goodness pass before you." So the Torah tells us that God placed Moses in the cleft of a rock and said: "As my presence passes by, I will shield you with my hand until I have passed by. Then I will take my hand away and you will see my back; but my face must not be seen."

So our ancestor Moses, the most religious of all human beings, finally acknowledges that it is not possible to know God directly, that human beings can only know God through reflections of God in our world, in nature, and within human beings. And Moses accepts that answer. His faith in God is rebuilt not through any direct experience of God, but through his struggle with his own doubts and his own willingness to choose between meaninglessness and meaningfulness, between denying that there is purpose to our world and affirming that we can make a difference in the way the world is. He sees only God's back, only reflections of God, but he knows.

So Moses carves two new tablets and inscribes the Ten Commandments on them. He returns to the people of Israel, having affirmed his faith in a God he could not know with certainty, but ready to stake his life on the value of those Ten Commandments as a reflection of God. He returns with only the understanding that human beings have to make choices, without certainty, and that doing so is what it means to believe in God.

The Torah tells us that Moses' face glowed when he came from Mt. Sinai, that his face was so radiant that the people could not look directly at him and so he veiled his face. We have all had a moment or two like that, when we glowed with the knowledge of the goodness and the potential of human life. And we, too, veil ourselves, hide behind another face, because such emotion seems childish, naïve, irrational and unscientific. But it is in those moments that we understand what it means to believe in God, and it is when we can do

Doubt

so, openly and unveiled, that we create God's presence among us. We are more religious than we know. And we can derive more strength from it than we might suspect.

Moses was, indeed, the greatest of all prophets. He struggled, he doubted, faltered … and then he made a choice. And his face was radiant.

JOY AND SORROW

The Torah says: After the in-gathering from your threshing floor and your vat, you shall hold the Festival of Booths for seven days. You shall rejoice in your festival with your son and daughter, your male and female slave, the Levite, the stranger, the fatherless, and the widow in your communities. You shall hold a festival for the Lord your God seven days, in the place that the Lord will choose; for the Lord your God will bless all your crops and all your undertakings and you shall have nothing but joy.

Somehow, this instruction to observe the holiday of *Succot* is not the most compelling of the commandments in the Hebrew Bible. *Succot* is sort of a troublesome holiday because, after *Selichot, Rosh Hashanah* and *Yom Kippur*, it feels like we have had just about enough of Jewish holidays for a while. We have wished to a thousand different people that they be inscribed in the Book of Life. We have both eaten

Joy and Sorrow

holiday dinners and felt the pangs of the fast. We have expressed our identities as Jews and made our peace with God. So we feel like we have done enough for a while, had enough of Jewish holidays. Then we find ourselves at *Succot*.

The Bible gives several different names for *Succot*, each emphasizing a different aspect of the festival. *Chag He'Asif*, the Festival of the In-gathering, reminds us that this holiday originally was a vibrant celebration of the fact that there would be enough food for the coming year. It was the festival of the harvest, a holiday for a people who worked in the fields day after day and who had finally, after months of back-breaking effort, come to see, quite literally, the fruits of their labor. They harvested their grain and their fruits and celebrated the fact that their tenuous existence had been provided for, for yet another year.

Succot is also called *Chag Adonai*, the Festival of the Lord. This name signifies the fact that the people knew that they had not achieved this sense of security completely by their own efforts. They knew they were beholden to the One who provided rain, sun, and other conditions favorable to the growth of the crops. But the community of ancient Israel could not just come to their neighborhood synagogues to praise God; there were no synagogues in ancient Israel. There was only the Temple in Jerusalem, which was believed to be the permanent dwelling place of the spirit of God. So the people made the pilgrimage to Jerusalem, coming from all over the land, three times a year – on Passover, on *Shavuot* and on *Succot* – *Chag Adonai*. On this holiday, the people made the long journey to Jerusalem to thank and praise God for the goodness of their harvests.

Finally, there is the name we are most familiar with, *Chag Ha-Succot*, the Festival of Tabernacles or Booths. This name reminds us that our ancestors wandered through the desert for forty years, dwelling in temporary fragile structures that barely protected them. They lived in those same temporary booths each year as they made the long journey to Jerusalem, to present their offerings of fruit and grain, and the sacrificial offerings, before God.

Succot also was known as *He'Chag*, the Festival, communicating the sense that this holiday was of the utmost importance to our ancestors, a holiday of supreme joy, security, and thankfulness.

Having reviewed these names and their meanings, the much smaller role the holiday of *Succot* plays in our contemporary lives becomes more clear. *Succot* cannot be for us what it was for our ancestors, for we are so removed from the context which gave birth to this celebration. We are removed from the land; we do not plant our crops, we do not see them come to fruition. Sometimes, we are so removed from the agricultural world that we do not even make the connections between the availability and price of certain fruits and vegetables in the grocery store, and the season, or the year's growing conditions. We walk into the grocery store and are annoyed when exactly what we want is not there at the price we want to pay for it. But we forget about the planting of seeds, the harvesting of crops. It is very difficult for us to celebrate a holiday devoted to harvest, when none of us actually harvests.

And can we imagine making the trek to Jerusalem, struggling to come a little bit closer to God's presence to express our joy at the knowledge that we will be sustained for another year? Can we imagine bringing offerings before God, making sacrifices to God, to express our thanks? These things are completely removed from our lives and the way we live them.

Generations of Jews throughout history have continued the tradition of building the booths, *succot*, and if not actually dwelling

Joy and Sorrow

in them, perhaps saying a blessing or even having a meal in them, and immersing themselves in the symbolism the booths present to us, but even this custom has faded. Many of us feel that we do not have the time or space to actually build and decorate a *succah*, so we have made *succah*-building a communal activity, something the synagogue does for us, a symbolic reminder of what was once a very personal symbol of reverence before God.

The path of history and our lives, the very development of Judaism itself, has led us away from the concepts behind *Succot*, from its imagery and its observance. What then, can be the significance of this festival?

Yesterday, I went to the hospital on my regular weekly visit. I walked into the room of a young woman who was very unsteadily making her way across the room, back to her bed, leaning for support on a large walking stick. As she settled herself back into bed, we made polite conversation about the surprising cold weather and uninspiring hospital food, and how generally rotten it was to be in the hospital. I was having a very hard time figuring out what was wrong with her. She was young, about 26, and quite beautiful and, aside from the walking cane, she looked the picture of health. We talked for some time, and I noted that she was working very hard to put me at my ease, instead of the other way around. She was cheerful and vivacious, and I was confused.

She finally said, "Rabbi, I don't tell this to many people, but I want you to know because I have some questions to ask you." She told me that she had multiple sclerosis and was in the hospital for a regular monthly treatment. She had had the disease for almost two years, and her body was slowly deteriorating. She looked at me out of cheerful, courageous eyes and said: "Rabbi, I'm O.K. I'm dealing with my illness. But here's the thing that worries me. Judaism was always so important to me – I believed in it, I practiced it, I always knew I would marry someone Jewish and have a Jewish home. But now," she said, "I'm growing away from all that. Judaism doesn't have any answers for me; Rabbis don't have anything to say to me. They can't tell me why this is happening to me and they can't tell me everything's going to work out. Jews can't even pray for me the way my Christian friends do. At least when they hold my hand and pray for me, I feel comforted. Rabbi, Judaism just doesn't mean anything to me anymore. It doesn't have any answers."

I sat for a long time, thinking, and holding her hand. I finally took a deep breath, swallowed hard and said: "Listen to me, Lynn. There are two kinds of religious people. There are people who come to religion looking for answers, demanding explanations: God, why did this happen to me? Why is the world the way it is? These people either develop a fundamentalist attitude toward religion, accepting the simple answers, or they reject religion completely.

"And there are people who come to religion *knowing* that there are no answers, knowing that the human mind is incapable of comprehending the reason for all the turmoil in the world. Such people bring a different attitude to their Judaism. We are all still looking for answers, but that search is no longer the primary task. Judaism becomes not a philosophy, not a way of trying to comprehend, but a way of trying to live. It becomes a way of insisting that we maintain our dignity as human beings and struggle all the time to emphasize the goodness in our lives and, more than that, to create that goodness. Judaism is a way of looking at all the evil in the world, even the misery in our own lives, and spitting at it in the eye. Judaism becomes a way of saying 'I'm not going to give up,' a way of affirming the good in the world. That's why

Joy and Sorrow

the cycle of holidays is so important, and that's why we make such a big deal out of life cycle events – births, and Bar Mitzvahs, and weddings. It is because every holiday and every *simcha*, regardless of its specific meaning, has an underlying purpose. It's a reason to be together with other people, a time to love and be loved, an excuse for celebration, a time to feel the joy of being alive and a time to affirm what is good."

We talked for a few more moments and I left. As I came down the elevator, I happened to bump into a friend who sadly told me that she had been visiting her fourteen year-old nephew, who had had a swimming accident and was paralyzed from the waist down. I felt like I had been hit with a double whammy and, as I drove home, did my best to remind myself of the words I had just spoken to Lynn. You cannot demand answers. You must affirm the goodness, the joy, in the face of the evil. That is what being religious is all about.

And so the last name the Bible gives us for the holiday of *Succot* is *Z'man Simchateynu*, the Season of Joy. It does not matter if our lives are not going along the way we would like them to, the way we were told they would when we were children. It does not matter if we are overworked and undernourished. It does not matter even if we are mourning a death. Even so, *Succot* says, as the New Year begins, find a way to be joyful. *Succot* celebrations took place in the ghettos of Europe and in pogrom-plagued Russia. No matter what else is happening in your life, *this* is the day of our joy.

The Rabbis note: "Isn't it odd that we celebrate this holiday devoted to joy not in the safe, secure confines of our comfortable homes, but in the *succah*, a frail, small, and unimpressive hut. The *succah* is decorated not with works of art but with simple, everyday objects of nature – apples and carrots and corn. Wouldn't it be easier to celebrate a truly joyous festival in more pleasant surroundings?

"Ah," the Rabbis respond, "easier, perhaps, but isn't it more important to celebrate a sense of joy under circumstances that are not so perfect? Imagine all the dreadful things that could affect someone trying to fully observe this holiday in the *succah*, someone who was eating and sleeping in the *succah* for seven days. Seven days of facing the possibility of rain soaking you and wind blowing at you. Seven days of heat and mosquitoes and gnats. Seven days of making yourself especially vulnerable to all kinds of trouble."

And *this* is Z'man Simchateynu, the Season of our Joy?

"Ah," the Rabbis respond further. "It is just so. It is to remind you, to prove to you, that the externals have nothing to do with joy. The daily events of your life have little to do with your responsibility to search for and experience a sense of joy. Despite sickness, financial difficulties, mourning, or dissatisfaction, the *succah* says to us, 'no matter how hard the wind may blow, we can still cope. We can still find the joy of being' in our fragile *succah*. The holiday of *Succot* says to us that while we have become used to certain comforts and securities, if need be, we could live in a *succah*. And, in doing so, we still can find joy."

So many things go wrong in the average life and we think we will not be able to cope. But, given rain and wind and heat and mosquitoes, I have never seen a *succah* fall. We are stronger than we think. And when we peel back the layers of frustration and doubt and concern we wrap ourselves in, we will find that the core of our beings is strong, just as the seemingly fragile *succah* is strong, strong enough to withstand all kinds of external trouble.

Where then, does this internal sense of joy stem from? What can we do to nourish and develop it, so that when our *succah* seems to be the most fragile, we will still be able to sense its beauty? One Rabbi suggests that the four elements making up the *lulav* and *etrog*, symbols

Joy and Sorrow

of this holiday of joy, are also symbols of the qualities we must develop within ourselves in order to nourish our own sense of joy.

First, we have the leaves of the palm tree. The palm is long and straight and proud. It is like a backbone for the *lulav*; it causes the *lulav* to stand tall with self-respect. The palm says to us: Your own self-respect is what will make you stand tall. Guard it, at all costs.

The myrtle leaves are said to symbolize the human eye, the eye we must train to see and appreciate the beauty in things, in people, in actions. The eye that can see beyond the surface level, perceive the way people behave, and understand that we are all plagued with doubts and insecurities that cause us to behave in something less than beautiful ways. The myrtle reminds us to look farther, to look deeper, in our search for the beauty.

The willow leaves are symbolic of the human mouth that must know how to sing, to praise, and to thank, that must be used to glorify all the joys we take for granted. The luxurious growth of the willow teaches us that we must never stop growing. We must always continue, striving for a new feeling of accomplishment.

The *etrog* itself is likened to a heart, a heart that feels and is sympathetic to others. A heart that makes a person look beyond his or her personal disappointments and fears, and become able to show real concern for another.

Self-respect, an eye that searches out beauty, a mouth able to sing and praise, a commitment to growth, a willingness to make the concerns of others our own. These are the qualities *Succot* reminds us we must develop in order to create *Z'man Simchateynu*, the Season of our Joy. But joy comes most of all from the symbol of the *Succah* itself, which, though it may look fragile, can withstand a great deal. The joy comes most of all from the knowledge that we can cope with life.

Leaning on God

A story is told of a very pious Jew who was not feeling well on *Succot*. Despite his wife's warning that he might catch a cold if he slept in the *succah*, he spent most of the holiday there, in accordance with the law – and promptly caught a cold. The wife chided her husband. "See what happened to you because you slept in the *succah*?" "You don't understand," the pious Jew retorted. "It's true that I'm ill because I fulfilled the commandment of dwelling in the *succah*. However, can you imagine how severe my illness would have been if I had not done my duty?"

As I thought about that, and prepared for the *Succot* service, I thought not about dwelling in booths, or pilgrimages to Jerusalem or wheat harvests. I thought about the instruction to rejoice in this festival with your son and your daughter, the stranger, the fatherless, the widow. I thought about the instruction to gather your community together to make an opportunity to share, to be together in joy and celebration, to make a happy occasion out of what could be just an ordinary day or a painful day. That is what *Succot* is about for us; that is why we need to be together to celebrate it. *Z'man Simchateynu*: the season of our joy. It is a chance for us to share something and to create something glorious in our lives. *Succot* does give us an opportunity to be together as a community and at the end of the service to wish one another a heartfelt *Chag Sameach*, a joyous holiday.

TRUST

The Flood of '93. It sounds like something old men sitting on the front porch would be telling stories about, something that probably happened in 1893. But it was just this summer that the waters of the Mississippi hit a new record-shattering crest just about every day or two, and nature confounded people who live on the banks of that mighty river, as the flood waters ravaged their homes and their lives. People stood by watching ten times the normal amount of rain fall for over two months, killing at least forty, immersing 13.5 million acres of land, causing an estimated $10 billion in damage. Next to houses under four feet of water stood sunburned families, their faces shocked, numbed, tormented, determined.

Nick and Crystal Goederis farm a 150-acre homestead near Quincy, Illinois, that has been in their family for 160 years. After moving out everything they owned, they defiantly spent one last night in their house, in sleeping bags, on the living room floor. "We didn't want to leave," said Crystal. "It was our home."

Jackie Meek, 40, said: "I see my house on the news, and I just cry."

Farmers stared at their ruined crops, children at their mud-filled homes, and I spent the summer thinking about where they all found the strength to keep going.

While Nick Goederis and Jackie Meek sandbagged, cleaned their houses, went to banks for loans, and tried to explain the power of nature to their children, I came upon a song that, for me, became a prayer. The prayer taught me something about faith, and what it means for a Jew to have faith. I began to understand that these devastated people *would* rebuild, as generations before them, in every country of the world, have rebuilt after catastrophe struck.

Here is the beginning of the song, words of faith and trust:

(Verse 1)

A baby child is born along the highway
A tiny little thing upon the land
And an Okie with his dreams out on the byway
He lifts the tiny baby in his hand.
The woman smiles a little smile of knowing
And whispers something softly in his ear
Perhaps a little prayer to help the growing
Perhaps a word of comfort through the tears.

(Chorus)

You trust the moon to move the mighty oceans
You trust the sun to shine upon the land
You take the little that you know

And you do the best you can
You see the rest with the quiet faith of man.*

Imagine, then, a poor man, on the road, with his wife, and a newborn baby. He does not know how he will care for that baby, how he will feed, or clothe it, how he will protect it. But he sings first of the rhythms of nature that he knows will continue. You trust the moon to move the mighty oceans. You trust the sun to shine upon the land.

In Hebrew, the word for this kind of trust, this faith, is *emunah*. *Emunah* is used in the Bible to describe the relationship of human beings to God, but it does not mean *belief* in God, as we might speak today about people who believe in God, or don't believe in God. It speaks of *trust* in God.

Somewhere in the Middle Ages, *emunah* was connected to belief in God, as rational proofs for the existence of God were vigorously argued. But in the Bible, to have *emunah*, faith, was to assert something about the nature of human existence and about the truths by which human beings live. *Emunah* was not a cognitive term. No one said: Prove to me that God exists. It was an emotional and responsive reaction to being alive.

As the song says, you take the little that you know – we know so very little about why things happen the way they do in human life, so little about what our ultimate purpose as human beings is – you take the little that you know – and you do the best you can.

The best you can at coping with this life, filling it with love and courage, even when it is inexplicably painful, especially when the pain cannot be understood.

---

* Jerry Jeff Walker, "Quiet Faith of Man." By Bill Staines. *Live at Gruene Hall.* RYKO, 1989. CD.

Leaning on God

And you see the rest with the quiet faith of man.

You act as witness to this world. Sometimes the best you can do is stand by silently, and acknowledge the events of this world, the events of our lives. Sometimes, most times, we can do nothing but witness, with the faith that nature will proceed, and somehow, so will we. So we quiet the rage in our souls, the panicked cries that we do not understand, the one-word indictment "Why?" that we long to scream out, and to have answered.

And we learn to see, to witness, with the quiet faith of man.

Where does this faith come from, this *emunah*, this trust?

It is somewhere in each one of us. I cannot tell you how to find it in you, or how it got there. But I know the potential for trust, for faith, is in each one of us. For me, it is literally in my gut; I feel it, as I square my shoulders and absorb sad news or shocking news. It is a ribbon of strength that gets pulled taut around me and supports me, as I relax against it, and am held up, instead of falling. Or a black hole in me, a protected place where fears and doubts do not hold sway. It radiates faith; its by-products are courage and strength.

It is in there. It is in me and it is in you.

In part, it is an awareness of a plane of existence way beyond our lives, against which we are a speck, a tiny piece of the humanity that stretches back so many generations and forward even more. It's the knowledge that, however tiny our speck is, at the very same time it is the necessary link to the future, to all future generations. We need to be here, each one of us, in all our glorious uniqueness, in all our joy and misery, in order for the future to be realized. We are the critical link to the future.

In part, it's a choice. You have to make a choice for faith. It's like a muscle that needs to be exercised to get strong. As with a muscle, when you exercise it, you feel it. There come moments when we are faced with a choice so big, and so small. At every crossroad, at every disappointment, disaster, and setback in our lives – and at every moment of joy as well, because they are so fleeting. These are moments when we can choose to exercise our faith by focusing on the ultimate nature of life, as we face the particular details of our own lives. Moments when, with a flash of insight, we grasp that it's not all about me – it's about aliveness, existence, the progress of humanity.

And then you realize you can continue.

And that realization allows you to re-focus on your own life – to face it, and make it good. To know what matters and what doesn't matter. To live with faith.

The second verse of the song tells us:

> A tractor makes its way along the fence line
> And drops the seeds precisely in a row
> If the rains are kind and the winds don't take the topsoil
> Before too long the crops will start to show.
> The farmer sees the fields around him growin'
> He whispers something low beneath his breath
> Perhaps a little prayer to help the growing
> Perhaps a word of thanks for all the rest.

The farmer's prayer to help the growing exercises the faith muscle. So does the word of thanks for all the good. But what happens when the rains aren't kind and the wind *does* take the top soil? What happens to all the farmers whose crops were ruined this year? What happens when you feel small, so small – when you are afraid – afraid to chant your Torah portion at your Bar Mitzvah; or that you will take another drink; or that you will suddenly cry in the middle of a normal conversation; or that you won't make enough money to support your family? What happens when you stare into the sunset and realize that the days ahead are shorter?

You make a choice for faith, trusting the cycles of nature, doing "the best you can . . . with the quiet faith of man."

There is always an ebb and flow in the life of faith. We lose faith and then we regain it. The faltering is balanced by a surge of *emunah*, and we hold steady.

There's a peculiar legend in the book of Exodus. When Moses was leading the Israelites in battle against Amalek, the Torah tells us he positioned himself on the top of a hill along with Aaron and Hur and he held the rod of God in his hand. Then, whenever Moses held up his hand, Israel prevailed, but whenever he let down his hand, Amalek prevailed. But Moses' hands grew heavy and he could no longer hold them up. So they took a stone and put it under him, and he sat on it, while Aaron and Hur, one on each side, supported his hands. The text says: "Thus his hands remained steady until the sun set."

In that sentence, the Hebrew word for steady is *emunah*. When we cannot be strong any longer, the force that comes along to hold us up, to keep us steady, is *emunah*. Faith is that which keeps us steady.

Again, this word comes, in the book of Isaiah. A particular man is being named leader of the house of Israel. God says: "I will give to him the key to the House of David. He shall open and none shall shut. He shall shut and none shall open. I will fasten him as a peg, in a firm place." There, the Hebrew word for firm is *enumah*. Like a peg, fastened into a wall, is the faith you can choose. A steady, strong faith. *Emunah*.

And the song tells us, at the end:

> There's a storm tossed ship tonight out on the ocean
> There's a soul somewhere adrift out on the blue

Trust

> There's a dreamer with his eye upon the heavens
> They're all looking for a way to make it through.

We are storm-tossed ships on the ocean, thrown from one wave in our lives to the next. We are souls adrift, and *anything* can happen to us. But, having this kind of faith is not related to what happens to you. It is related to who you are, how you live, how you respond to being tossed around like a ship in a stormy ocean. Sometimes, it all looks so tenuous, but we have the capacity to be so strong, like the thinnest strand of silk that is yet extraordinarily resilient.

Yet another word is related to *emunah*. You hear in it the same letters which form the word: Amen. Amen means: so be it. We say it at the end of prayers to express agreement.

To live with faith is to witness, and witness all that happens – all that we don't understand; all that pains us. To find the strength to do the best we can, and to say: Amen. So be it.

On this first day of a new year, feel the strength, the steadiness of *choosing* to have faith. Then, regardless of what happens, between this *Rosh Hashanah* and the next, the year will be sweet. The chorus comes back to remind us:

> You trust the moon to move the mighty oceans
> You trust the sun to shine upon the land
> You take the little that you know
> And you do the best you can
> You see the rest with the quiet faith of man.

IV
CHANGE AND RITUAL

LEANING ON GOD, PART II: SAYING GOODBYE
(1986)

It never occurred to me when I came to Houston, to Congregation Beth Israel, that I would ever look out over the congregation and see the faces of friends. When I came, there was only an unidentifiable mass of strange faces out there staring back at me with which it was nearly impossible to connect. Now, three years later, I treasure the first moments of every *Shabbat* service, when I look out and know I will see Shep and Beverly over on the right side and Carole and Howard more towards the middle and Harvey and Sandy, and Norman and Berne, all in a row up in front. I take note of people who are usually here but are not, and wonder if they are sick, or out of town, or just too tired; and I am amused by those who are usually not here, but

Leaning on God

who are, and wonder if they are related to the Bar or Bat Mitzvah family, or have a *Yahrtzeit* I did not know about, or are just in need of a pause and some comfort.

When did it happen that the sea of strangers became identifiable, individual people whose lives I know and by whom I am known?

That process of watching the unknown become known describes, better than anything else, what it is I have been doing here these three years, and what I have learned. I came to Houston three days after my 26th birthday, 16 days after having been ordained as rabbi. I knew no one in Houston, nothing about Houston, and had never had a full-time job. Just as the sea of strangers became known individuals, Houston became familiar and appreciated. I made deep connections with people here, and I became a Rabbi. It was hard and uncomfortable and painful, for a long time. And then it became known and dear.

Now I am about to expose myself to the other side of the equation, to deal with a complete and total unknown again, and it is frightening. But the first of the thoughts I want to leave you with tonight is that we learn the *most* valuable things in our lives from that unknown, from surviving until the unknown becomes known. Whether it comes from changing a job or becoming a grandparent or moving or becoming Jewish or losing someone, these transitions are when we learn the most about ourselves and what it is we are doing here in this life we live. And it is uncomfortable, if not painful, and we ask "why me? – this isn't the way my life was supposed to be" – and, for a time, we do not recognize our own lives, and it is frightening.

We have to go through the uncomfortable part in order to keep doing our human task, in order to evolve, to understand more. I used to think that what I wanted out of life was to be content; now

Saying Goodbye

I believe there is another level on which we must be functioning, a level of challenge and discomfort which inevitably leads to deeper understanding. As an article of faith, I now know that there is something to be learned from *everything* that happens to us. The relevant question is not "Did I do the right thing?" or "Did I make the right decision?" or "How do I survive this?" The only question is: "What is the universe trying to teach me through this, and am I able to learn it?" I do not say that this learning justifies the suffering we have to go through; I say only that it is possible to see every experience on another level.

I think of our legend of Adam and Eve, of how safe and secure these human beings were in the Garden of Eden. All their needs were provided for, they were surrounded by beauty and calm, and they were content. The Torah tells us that Adam and Eve were told not to eat the fruit of one particular tree in the Garden, and they disobeyed that command. They were punished by being banished from the Garden and afflicted with a variety of human difficulties. One modern commentator, however, sees this familiar story a bit differently, and writes a *midrash* asking: Were Adam and Eve, in fact, punished by their banishment from the Garden of Eden? He answers with a different interpretation. Adam and Eve were aimlessly wandering around the Garden one day, when, through a hole in the fence, they saw a small, scraggly, undernourished-looking little tomato plant. They were amazed, because they never had seen anything look so, so sick and sad and needy, because everything in the Garden was perfect. Every day, they would go and look at the tomato plant, which only got worse and worse looking. One day they said to God: "We want to go help it. We have never seen anything so sick and sad before," but God told them, "If you choose to leave the Garden, you can *never* come back. Think of everything *else* that's out there. *This* is the perfect world." Adam and Eve took another long look at the tomato plant, turned on their heels and walked right out of the Garden and nursed that little tomato plant back to life.

Under this *midrash*, Adam and Eve were not punished by being kicked out of the Garden of Eden; they chose to leave because they perceived that, without a challenge, without something to learn from, their lives were purposeless. So they left the Garden, where they were content, to face the world, where we as their offspring are constantly challenged, where things and people die and are sick and just plain hurt. And they knew the trade-off was worth it.

The trade-off *is* worth it. We must be uncomfortable to keep progressing. And we must keep progressing to be fully human, to be fully alive.

Many of you were here the night of my first sermon. I remember walking down the hallway and entering the back of the sanctuary with Rabbi Karff, from whom I have learned so much. I stood and stared at this marble lectern and at the six or seven hundred people sitting in here. I turned and looked at Sam and said: "Oh boy." He said something along the lines of, "Now's the time to lean on your faith in God." I did not know what he meant. Despite all my studies of theology and philosophy and God language, I did not know how to draw on a personal relationship with that which is sacred in order to give me strength.

After three years of living with this congregation – of experiencing the hospital stays and the funerals and the births and the weddings and the committee meetings and the parties – I think I know better what he meant. I have different ways of defining God and I know more about how to draw strength from that which I call God. It has to do with having experienced the life cycle over and over again, through all of your lives. Somehow, seeing those patterns fall into place makes me look at human life from a distance. It makes me know that we experience life on two different levels: the microcosm, where we live each moment of our lives as if it were the only moment, when the particular events of our lives are paramount and can be unbearably joyful or overwhelmingly painful; and the macrocosm, where we know that there are hundreds of thousands of years for the pattern of life to make sense, and that our task is to keep the life process flowing forward. God becomes, then, the faith that, in the long run, it will make sense, that regardless of what happens in a *particular* moment of *our* lives, the universe is working and, on a much larger plane, it will come out right. Working towards that end, filling the world with actions and emotions that are positive, and nurturing and moving humanity forward, is what makes our world sacred.

I am *so* careful about changing the God language in our prayer book from the all-masculine "He's" and "Him's" and "King's" to the simple word God, not because I think God is a she or because our prayer book is so anti-female, but to remind us that our faith should be much more profound than to deal with an image of God that is so limited. I change the language to remind us that God is completely beyond what we can conceive of – and that we are able to draw strength from God when we ally ourselves with all that is sacred and alive in the universe. My God is not a he – my God is *knowing* that it all makes sense. My God is believing that we do not have to be limited by the pictures in our minds or by the standards and perceptions with which we were raised. My faith is knowing that we can, at any moment, make a decision to make the world the way we want it, the way *we* think it should be. We determine the way the world is by our own behavior. One way of drawing strength from one's faith in God at a difficult or painful moment is to have faith in the sacred progression of life; we can know that, in the very long run, there are patterns to what happens to us, and that it will all come out right.

Some of you know that I love country music, and even loved it long before I ever came to Texas. My most favorite performer, Jerry Jeff Walker, wrote a song some years ago about being a singer/songwriter. I think Jerry Jeff Walker and I are soul mates; he captured the way I feel about being a Rabbi. He wrote:

> Layin' my life on the line
> That's what I do all the time.
> I find myself each night
> Facing a white light
> Layin' my life on the line.*

This congregation has made it possible for me to lay my life on the line, over and over again. You have allowed me to be so vulnerable because you have been willing to take what I have offered. You have listened, and cared about the things I have said. You have allowed me to learn how to say what is true for me and not be afraid that it will be rejected because it is imperfect or awkward or difficult to hear. You have allowed me to learn how to be a leader, showed me that the times I kept silent taught me, and others, the least. And you have reminded me that it is all right to make mistakes, that it is so much more important to go ahead and *do* something – badly, if you must – rather than be immobilized by the fear that what you do won't be good enough.

---

* Todd Snider, "Layin' My Life on the Line." *Time As We Know It: The Songs of Jerry Jeff Walker.* Aimless Records, 2012. CD.

Saying Goodbye

We are all so much better off when we allow each other to lay our lives on the line.

In several weeks I will be in California, and you will be in Houston. I will have a new congregation, and you will have a new Rabbi. But we do not lose each other now, because we have all learned together. We are changed for having known one another, and a connection remains.

I want to end with a blessing. I want to us say the *shechecheyanu* together. I know it is an odd time for a *shechecheyanu*, but to be thankful at a moment of departure is to say that this time was precious, and that there is reason to thank God for it. It is also to assert the faith that the newness, the unknown to come for all of us, will also be valuable and precious.

Baruch atah adonai, elohenu melech ha'olam, shechecheyanu, v'keamanu, v'higeanu, l'azeman hazeh.

Praised are you our God, Ruler of the universe, for giving us life, for sustaining us, and for enabling us to reach this precious moment.

Amen.

SAYING HELLO
(1986)

I have been imagining this moment for weeks now. I imagined it with joy, with fear, with excitement, with trepidation. I imagined it with such a sense of loss for all that I have left behind that I winced from the pain, and with such a sense of joyful expectation of what is to come, that I have felt myself glow with the pleasure of it. I have imagined this moment, as the people of Israel, wandering in the wilderness for so long, imagined their arrival at the land of Israel. I have imagined looking out over your faces, mostly unknown to me, a sea of strangers, and I have imagined the process that will now begin to take place, the incredible life-affirming, sacred process, of watching the unknown become known.

Many times, I have doubted the wisdom of leaving, of changing, of uprooting, just as the Israelites complained to Moses: "Why have you taken us away from Egypt, where we had meat to eat, and plenty to drink, where we were safe, where we were known, why have you taken us to this wilderness, to die?" I never understood their cry, as I do now. But never before have I seen so clearly, understood with such faith, that it is in uprooting, in changing, in creating an unknown in our lives, and then making it known, that we really come alive. It is on the journey that it happens, that *we* happen. Forty years the Israelites wandered, from Egypt to Israel; let me tell you, they took the long way around. But the point was not to get there; the point was the journey, to make the unknown become known and thereby surely to encounter God's presence. With that thought in mind, I look out over your faces, strange and unknown, and I feel the panic in me subside. I cherish the chance we now have, to let our lives intertwine, to become known to each other, to embark together on a new journey.

"What can I tell them about me," I thought, as I imagined all this. "What can I tell them that will bridge the gap, that will bring these two unknown entities closer to one another?"

There are three questions I get asked with some regularity. The first two are easy. The third is a bit more complicated.

Number one: You are the first woman Rabbi I ever met; how many women Rabbis are there? Answer: I have lost count at this point, but I would say there are somewhere around 115 ordained women Rabbis. Rabbi Sally Priesand was the first in America; she was ordained in 1972. At this point, the student body of the Hebrew Union College is fully one-half women. The Conservative movement has ordained one woman and several others are quite close to completing their requirements for ordination. So having women Rabbis is quietly becoming an accepted element in American Jewish life.

Leaning on God

Question number 2, also easy: If the Rabbi's wife is called the *rebbetzin*, what do you call the husband of the woman Rabbi? Answer: lucky.

Question number 3, the not so easy one, usually asked in a tone of voice that mixes skepticism and awe. What made you want to become a Rabbi?

For me, the decision to become a Rabbi was part of a long, slow process. I know I was already thinking about it, at the time of my own Bat Mitzvah, which is odd because there were no women Rabbis yet. But that thought never occurred to me. I grew up in Washington D.C., the youngest of five children. My mother was the first woman president of our congregation, and we kids grew up not being really clear which was our living room – the one at home or the Sanctuary at Temple. We followed our mother's footsteps in being active at Temple. We sang in the choir, went to Sunday school, participated in the youth group. My family is what I like to call Observant Reform. We did not follow all the traditions; we decided which traditions we would follow based on what was meaningful to us. We never kept kosher, yet we always had Shabbat dinner, complete with white tablecloth and blessings and a discussion of the Torah portion. Jewish tradition threaded itself in and out of our lives and I never doubted for a moment that all the important values that shaped me as a human being came from the tradition.

As is the case for most of us, decisions in my life were the result of painful experiences as well as joyful ones. My father died when I was 13, six months after my Bat Mitzvah. My mother remarried not long after and my stepfather died six years later, when I was 19. Through it all, the Rabbi was there, immediately, filled with loving, genuine, caring support. He was full of information about Jewish

Saying Hello

traditions that eased the way for us. I remember so clearly the Rabbi's coming to our home before my father's funeral. I know now that he was gathering information for a eulogy. I also know that, as he drew us out, as we remembered and shared stories, mixing laughter and tears, somewhere the knowledge began to sink in that healing could take place, that there was joy as well as sorrow in remembering that we would survive. Later, as I thought about what I wanted to do with my life I thought "What better than to do for other people what my Rabbi did for me? What better than to have access to people's lives when they are the neediest, at funerals and weddings, at births and Bar/Bat Mitzvahs? What better than to be a representative of all that our tradition has to offer, to ease these times of transition?"

Once in a while, after that, I entertained thoughts of doing something else with my life, of being a doctor or a lawyer or a country western singer – this is the only one I still think about sometimes! – but it seemed like the decision was made. I knew, the way you know very few things in your life, that this was what I needed to do.

So I studied philosophy at the University of Maryland and went directly to Hebrew Union College, in the rabbinic program. Nine long years later, four in college and five at HUC, the thought continued to cross my mind, and people often said: "Gosh, you could have been a doctor by now, with all that school," and I would shake my head sadly, and look at my bank book sadly and say "I know, I know," but I also know that being a Rabbi was what my life was about.

I was ordained in 1983, 13 days before my 26th birthday, and accepted a position as assistant rabbi of Congregation Beth Israel in Houston, Texas, an 1,800 family mega-temple where I had the opportunity to work with Rabbi Samuel Karff for three years. I hope you will all have the opportunity to meet Rabbi Karff soon. His wisdom and strength taught me so many things you cannot learn in school. With him, and with the tremendous amount of experience you get in a congregation so huge, I became a Rabbi in heart and soul, as well as in title.

"These are the facts I can share," I thought, "but what I really must tell them is what I care about." Because that is what a congregation is all about, a place where people talk about what they care about. We should be able to take the learning and the loving we get here out into the world with us, both as a gift to the rest of the world and as a protective coating which sustains us when the world out there bats us around a bit.

So what do I care about? Three main things, which I will highlight only very briefly, as I noticed at this point in my writing, that I had only two pages and two lines left. (You will find that another thing I care about very deeply is a strict limit of eight pages, tops, per sermon. And now I have only two pages left.)

First, the principle, the belief, on which I base all else: Human beings are created in God's image and are, therefore, unique, valuable, to be cherished, to be treated with love and respect. Each and every one of us. Uncle Sol, whom you only see at funerals; the guy down the street who plays his music too loud; the refrigerator salesman I nearly murdered when he said my refrigerator would not be delivered until Sunday; your husband; the woman who always talks too much about things she doesn't know anything about. Each one. Because one of the places we encounter God's presence is in each other, if we could only learn to do so.

Second – and this one deserves at least ten sermons – in order to grow religiously, we must rid ourselves of the lingering notion that God is a superhuman being, an old man with a long white beard

Saying Hello

who sits on a throne in heaven and manipulates occurrences here on earth. It sounds silly, but it is so, so easy, to fall back into that way of thinking that we are taught as children. But when we do that, we allow the fundamentalists to define the word God for us, when there are so many other ways for us to fill up the word God, so many other images we can use, to represent that which we believe is sacred in the universe. God, as a source of strength, as a Rock, as the creator, as that which is completely other, beyond us, beyond what we can conceive, that from which we are able to draw strength when we ally ourselves with all that is sacred and progressive and alive in the universe.

Third, it is our responsibility and our privilege and our glory as Jews to filter these two things – the Godliness of the individual and the all-encompassing nature of God – through our tradition, through Torah. It is through studying and learning, and reading and talking and interpreting our ancient texts that we learn the wisdom of our ancestors and become able to add to it. We read of the people's thirst for water from the Torah, and water has always been a symbol for Torah itself. Torah is called *Mayim Chaim* – the water of life, to strengthen roots, to refresh, to nourish.

I am a Rabbi, a teacher and a leader. This is my first step in becoming known to you. You are a community of Jews, whom I am waiting, impatiently, to come to know.

May we encounter God together. May we go from strength to strength. Within these walls, may we laugh, learn, love, live, nourish ourselves and one another, create God's presence in our midst: may we become holy.

AN EARLY WOMAN SCHOLAR

Her name was Beruriah. She is the only woman whose scholarly opinions are mentioned with respect in the Talmud. Although Beruriah was unusual and remarkable, her achievements have not been honored and her story has not been told. The tradition simply did not know what to make of her, for she was an enigma and she was threatening. So, as we honor those women who devote so much of themselves to making our congregation a home, it seems right that we should learn something about *this* woman, Beruriah, who so many hundreds of years ago made a place for herself as a leader in the Jewish world.

Beruriah had an advantage over most women of her time. She was the daughter of a thoughtful and famous Rabbi, Hananina Ben Teradyon who, incidentally, was martyred in the Bar Kochba war of

135. She also was the wife of Meir, another greatly renowned Rabbi of the time. As a result, she had the opportunity for something most women did not: a superb education. But it was Beruriah herself who had the qualities that allowed her to use these circumstances to her best advantage. She studied so seriously, and with such positive results, that she was held up as a role model to other aspiring scholars.

A story is told in the Talmud of a certain Rav Simlai who wanted to study with Rabbi Yochanan. Simlai said: "You must teach me this whole book within three months." Yochanan replied: "Hah, if Beruriah, wife of Meir and daughter of Teradyon, who studied 300 laws from 300 teachers in one day could not fulfill the duty of learning this book in three years, how do you propose to do so in three months?"

From this small piece, we learn much about Beruriah. She was a great student and a serious scholar, and took learning upon herself as a *duty*. Traditionally, in Judaism only men have a duty to study; women *may* study, but are not required to. Women have other duties, such as keeping a kosher home and keeping the laws of family purity, but certainly *not* the duty to study. Beruriah is the first woman we know of who said that learning and studying were duties that women ought to take upon themselves, no matter what the tradition said.

Beruriah developed a reputation first as a scholar, then as a teacher. Her teaching, they said, was full of compassion and concern for her students. But in this Talmudic passage, we see another side of Beruriah, a side of her that was immensely ironic and frustrated with the tradition's attitudes toward women.

Rav Yose the Galilean was once on a journey when he met Beruriah. "By what road," he asked her, "do we go to Lydda?" "Foolish Galilean," she replied, "did not the Rabbis teach 'Engage not in much talk with women?' You should have asked: 'By which to Lydda,' and thereby saved three words!" Surely Beruriah is registering her opposition to the rabbinic teaching against much talk with women, but she manages to do it with grace and patience, and from the inside. She shows her disdain for the law by using her superior knowledge of it, and by her sense of humor. One certainly gets the message that you could learn a bit from further talk with her.

In a similar interaction with her husband Meir, Beruriah is much less sarcastic, as she herself is clearly accepted as an equal by him. Meir was furious with some highwaymen who were causing trouble in their neighborhood, and he prayed that they should die. She said to him: "Surely you say this prayer on the basis of the verse "let sins, *hahaim*, cease." "But husband," she said, "the text says *hahaim*, sins, not *hotim*, sinners, and I know that at the end of the verse it says and 'let wicked men be no more.' But surely when the sins cease, there will be no more wicked men. So pray that they should repent, and there will be no more wickedness." He did pray for them, and they repented. Thereby Beruriah caused Meir to fulfill the words of God who said, "It is not the death of sinners I seek, but that they should turn from their ways, and seek good."

Even in tragedy, Beruriah tried to teach. Beruriah and Meir had two sons, and one Sabbath, both sons died. When her husband completed Havdalah, she said to him "Some time ago a certain man came and left something in my trust. Now he has called for it. Shall I return it to him or not?" Naturally, Meir said: "Of course," whereupon Beruriah showed him their dead children. When Meir began to weep, she said: "Did you not tell me that we must give back what was given on trust? God has given; God has taken away."

Beruriah was, then, a scholar and a person of faith—an impressive role model for both women and men. But as there is often a

An Early Woman Scholar

backlash against strong and successful women, later commentators apparently had a need to discredit Beruriah. Some 1,000 or so years after Beruriah lived, Rashi relates the following legend of unknown origin: once Beruriah scoffed at the rabbinical saying "Women are lightheaded," and her husband warned her that her own end might yet testify to the truth of the words. To put her virtue to the test, he charged one of his disciples to try to seduce her. After repeated efforts, she yielded, and then shame drove her to commit suicide. Rabbi Meir, tortured by remorse, fled from his home.

Where did this legend come from? We do not know. Is it true? We do not know. We can only hope not and reason that, from everything else we know about both Beruriah and Meir, it is unlikely. It seems more likely that a segment of the community was so uncomfortable with her great stature and tremendous recognition that the story was fabricated.

True or not, we know that Beruriah was a victim of her time. We know that she must have been extraordinary and brilliant to have accomplished as much as she did under the circumstances and that, had she been unencumbered, she may have achieved much more. She paved the way for the accomplishments of later generations of women, those who have had more of a chance to do as they see fit with their lives and their intellects. Many have chosen to give of themselves to this congregation and they have become the backbone of our congregation.

May the spirit of Beruriah continue to inspire and guide us. May we know how greatly we are blessed by having women in our community who follow in her footsteps.

AN EARLY WOMAN LEADER

I have found myself thinking a good deal about names. They are the ultimate symbol – just a single word, a few letters put together, that bring to mind a whole universe of associations, images, feelings and memories. You get a message of just two words, say, "Ruth called" and your day is made, because just the name evokes so many associations that are good and full of affection and pleasure. Or, say the opposite, say "Joe called" and you have been avoiding Joe for weeks now, and the reality behind that simple three-letter word fills you with anxiety and distress. Just a name creates an entire reality.

This being President's weekend, I have been thinking especially about two names, Lincoln and Washington, and I have been surprised at how much they mean to me. I have never seriously studied the lives of either of these two men, but, even so, their names are filled with associations. Abraham Lincoln – slavery, freedom, the Civil War, a country being torn apart. When you are a Jew reading the book of Exodus, you cannot help but think of the legend of our people's enslavement, and of how personal the principle of standing against slavery is, to each and every one of us. The name Lincoln stands for that – whether in reality or in the legend which grew up; just the name "Lincoln" means, as he said in the Gettysburg Address, that *all* human beings are created equal.

And Washington. Again, the facts and the legend merge, but we *feel* like he, alone, *was* the founder of this country. We say the name and call to mind our first president, and think of a symbol of hope, new possibilities, democracy, honesty, patriotism – all that the United States stands for. George Washington – just a name, a symbol of all the potential the idea of our country holds.

Just as powerful are the associations on the other side of that coin – Nixon, Watergate, Vietnam. Just names, but they pull up so many images that affect us so deeply.

We need to remember names and what they stand for in order to have heroes and role models. One of the hardest things about being one of the first women Rabbis is that there were no role models. There were no names, no symbols, to show how it can be done – or even that it *can* be done.

There are, in fact, very few role models in our community for liberal religious people, Jews who take holiness and ritual and spirituality seriously, yet are not bound to Orthodox ways. Some of our parents served as models, maybe some of our grandparents, maybe a teacher, or a friend. But we need the *names*, we need the symbols, to evoke that possibility.

In and among all these events is one simple statement in the *parasha* that riveted my attention: "The Israelites arrived at the

Wilderness of Zion on the first new moon and the people stayed at Kadesh. There, Miriam died and was buried." The text does not miss a beat; Miriam's death is simply announced and recorded. But in its terse, compact style, the Torah is telling us something important here. It is telling us that Miriam was a leader in Israel, that her death was significant because her life was significant.

I wish I could say that Miriam was one of the names I knew, one of my role models as I grew up and learned the stories of the Bible, but she was not. She was not because, as with most Biblical characters, it was hard to put together a whole picture of who Miriam was and what she had accomplished. The Torah reports only the smallest bits of information about Miriam's life and yet, the fact that she, being a woman, is mentioned at all, makes her unusual, and, one would assume, noteworthy. So what is it that Miriam did that has made her a name worth remembering? What is her name to symbolize for us; what kind of a role model might she be?

Here is the little that the Bible tells us about Miriam. It is Miriam who watches when her brother, the baby Moses, is floated down the Nile River and it is Miriam's suggestion to Pharaoh's daughter, who finds Moses, that a Hebrew nurse could suckle the baby, thereby insuring that Moses' mother would be there to raise him. We do not hear of Miriam again until years later, when the Israelite people cross the Red Sea into freedom, and it is Miriam, as I earlier read from the Torah, who now is puzzlingly referred to as the prophetess, and who leads the women in triumphant song. In one final episode Miriam challenges the decisions and authority of Moses during the wandering in the desert, and for this she is punished with an outbreak of leprosy.

On the surface, that is all we know about Miriam, and yet our tradition has deemed her important enough to have included her in the Torah, to speak of her with great honor, to have made her a role model, one of the few important women in the ancient texts. Who was she? What does her name mean?

The ancient Rabbis struggled with this issue as well, and the result of their struggle was a series of *midrashim*, stories they wrote as they imagined what Miriam must have been like, to deserve the honor attributed to her in the Torah. Their stories present a much fuller portrait of this unusual woman. They portray a fearless, active, determined, strong person, who was able to do things no other woman of her time could do.

A modern writer of *midrash*, frustrated by the still-fragmented and incomplete understanding of Miriam presented by the Rabbis, shaped all the bits and pieces of information and stories we have about Miriam into a whole. He chose to accomplish this by writing what he saw as a more fitting eulogy for Miriam than the one line which appears in the Torah, "And Miriam died and was buried there."

I asked him: "Why a eulogy of all things? Why not simply reconstruct Miriam's life story and leave it at that?" He said, "I want to learn how to mark a death not only with my own sorrow, focusing only on the loss, but also with joy, paying tribute, giving honor, to the immense beauty of the life that was lived. I wanted to write a eulogy for Miriam which would bring comfort to her mourners by reminding them just how blessed they were to have had such a person in their lives, so that they could praise God with the words of the *Kaddish* as they were intended to, instead of cursing God as we are all tempted to, at the time for eulogy giving." "Eulogies," he said, "are the greatest tributes we can offer, when they remove our focus from the pain of our loss, and place it instead on the beauty of the gift of life."

Leaning on God

*Miriam bat Amram v'Yocheved**

Miriam, daughter of Amram and Yocheved, sister of Moses and Aaron, died quietly in her sleep at the Israelite camp at Kadesh on the First day of Nisan, 2484. She was 123 years old when she passed away. She is survived by her husband, Caleb ben Jephuneh and seven children, among whom was Hur, the grandfather of the great artisan and builder of the Temple, Bezalel.

Miriam gained distinction at an early age when she prophesied the birth of her brother Moses and his deliverance of the Israelite nation from slavery, and insured the fulfillment of the prophecy by saving Moses' life at the waters of the Nile. When others would have let fate take its course, Miriam the prophetess recognized the need to protect that which she held most dear. It was no accident that Pharaoh's daughter found the baby Moses, nor that his mother, Yocheved, was brought to nurse him. Remember Miriam the brave; remember Miriam the strong.

Miriam was known by other names, most important of which was Puah, and it was with this name that she guaranteed the survival of the people as a whole, by serving with her mother as a midwife and disobeying Pharaoh's decree to kill all Israelite males. With flashing eye and flushed face, Miriam had raised her hand and, pointing to the Pharaoh on his throne, cried out: "Woe unto this man when the day of

---

* By Rabbi Norman J. Cohen, Ph.D., Provost *Emeritus*, Hebrew Union College--Jewish Institute of Religion, c. 1980.

An Early Woman Leader

retribution comes. God will punish him for his evil deed." Fearing the Pharaoh's anger, she worked to save Israelite children under a new name, Puah. Remember Miriam the brave; remember Miriam the strong.

Miriam's greatest moment came at the Red Sea when, like her famous younger brother Moses, she led the people in a messianic song as they passed through the redemptive waters. She danced and sang, full of the joy of life, full of hopes for the future of humankind. Remember Miriam the brave; remember Miriam the strong.

Miriam was willing to stand upon her principles, no matter what the consequences. Even though she suffered greatly, she was not afraid to call Moses to task for becoming consumed with his own leadership and power. Inflicted with leprosy, she would have been left behind in the wilderness, as the Israelites pushed on with their journey. The people were breaking camp and starting on the march when, upon turning to see the pillar of cloud which had led them, they missed the sight of it. They looked again to see if Moses and Aaron were in the line of procession, but they, too, were missing. God had remembered Miriam the brave, Miriam the strong, and the people were obliged to return to camp where they remained until Miriam was healed. Then the pillar of cloud moved on once more and the people knew that they had not been permitted to proceed on their march only because of this pious prophetess.

If you doubt the contribution made by this great leader of our people, then recall the fact that the well of water which gave Israel sustenance during their forty-year trek through the desert was present only because of her deed and that it disappeared at the moment of her death. God wrought this great miracle for the merits of the prophetess Miriam. And so it was called "Miriam's Well." Remember Miriam the strong; remember Miriam the brave.

Miriam, leader of Israel, triumphant singer of its messianic song, and mother who helped her children pass through the foreboding waters and reach the promised land, will always be remembered by us.

Zecher Tzadikah Livracha; may her memory be a blessing upon us.

And so, with this eulogy, the story has been filled out. We have a name, Miriam, and its associations: bravery and strength. May this name and its associations continue to grow, to stand as a role model for further generations.

HOMELESSNESS

On one of the routes I drive quite often, there is a freeway off ramp that has become the workplace for a particular woman. She sits there, almost every day, with a large cardboard sign that says "Help me and Joe with work or spare change." She sits and reads and smokes. Her dog sits next to her. I haven't figured out yet whether he's Joe.

Several times a week, I drive past and see her there, and the quandary in my soul grows. What is my responsibility to her? The Torah text seems pretty clear: you shall enjoy, together with the stranger in your midst, all the bounty that the Lord your God has bestowed upon you and your household. Surely I have been blessed with great bounty, and I do feel commanded to share it with those who do not have.

So why do I, like many other people I see there, stare straight ahead, keep the window rolled up tightly and stay in the middle lane, so I can tell myself that no one could be expected to reach over a lane of traffic to give a dollar or two? Although we feel commanded to give, and many of us make annual donations to organizations that try to meet the needs of homeless and hungry people, it is another thing to be faced every day with many different individuals, putting out their hands, asking for change. Sometimes they are scary, and we feel a bit threatened by them. Sometimes there are so many of them, especially for those of us who are often downtown, that it feels useless to give a dollar here or a dollar there; what will we do when we see the next one, and the next one, and the next one? Sometimes, if the truth be told, they arouse feelings of anger and resentment in us. "Why does she think she can sit there reading her book and expect passers-by to support her?" Or, "She'll probably just go spend it on liquor anyway," or any one of the many ways we manage to distance ourselves from these people, convincing ourselves that their problems are their own.

But, as we have been taught, their problems are not solely their own, and so, occasionally, we do give and, when we do not, we are consumed with conflict and guilt.

A bit of Talmud sheds some light. There was a poor man who begged from door to door and Rav Papa paid no attention to him. (It seems that Rav Papa shared some of *our* concerns.) So Rav Samma, the son of Rav Yiba, said to him, "If you pay no attention to him, then no one will, and he may starve to death." (This is our worst fear in that situation – that because *we* did not do *our* part, something drastic will happen.) "But is there not another ruling," Rav Papa said, "that teaches us that if a man begs from door to door, the community has nothing to do with him?" Rav Samma replied: "This ruling is simply trying to tell us that he should not be given a large amount, but a small contribution should be made."

This ruling implies that giving to individual beggars, one by one, is not the best way to go about supporting those in need. It means to say that we must give in a more logical, organized way. Most Rabbinic opinions agree that this should be a percentage of your annual income, which you decide upon at the beginning of the year. This way, you are assured all throughout the year that you are giving enough, and that you will not wait for the fortuitous moment when your heart is moved by some charity or another, but will give simply because it is the right thing to do.

So the Talmud is telling us that if you give in a regular way, then you should feel okay if you give the individual beggar on the street only a little something. It acknowledges the suspicion and fear we might feel towards individuals who are asking for money, and recognizes that we cannot support every needy person we see, but neither can we allow ourselves to become *so* hardened that we walk right by and do not allow ourselves to feel and to care. So we are taught to give a little something. The best advice I have heard is to decide how much per month you can afford to give in this way, keep that money in single bills in a special place, and when it is used up, you have done your share for that month.

Finally there is a notion in the Jewish concept of *tzedakah*, or charity, that a community has a responsibility to support its own beggars. If you go as a visitor to downtown San Francisco or to Los Angeles, for that matter, and you are overwhelmed by the nameless, faceless number of needy people there, you need not feel that it is your responsibility to do something for each of them. But when you pass someone often, when you know her face, when she is a regular part of your world, you dare not ignore her. She is a part of your community. If you do not acknowledge her, your heart will become too hardened for our tradition, for our souls, to bear.

So all my rationalizations aside – even if organizations ought to be supporting the lady I pass by so often; even if she is somehow taking advantage of me; even if I cannot support every beggar – I know now that I will start giving her something, each week, for my sake as much as for hers. May we not allow our hearts to become hardened to the pains of those about us; may we give as generously, and as whole-heartedly, as we can.

WRESTLING WITH RITUAL

Ever since Reform Judaism was born, there has been this complicated question of how much ritual a liberal Jew ought to do, to be considered responsible to the covenant. Now those two words, ritual and covenant, almost seem to be incompatible. The covenant itself is the pact our ancestors made with God, and which we continue to make simply by calling ourselves Jewish. It calls us to be true to God, and we have most often seen this "true-ness" in ethical and moral terms. If we are good, we are being Godly. If we remember that all human beings were created in the image of God, and therefore are Godly themselves, and if we treat them accordingly, then we are being true to the covenant.

We most often think of the terms of the covenant as being expressed in the Ten Commandments, nine of which can actually be seen as ethical or moral commandments. Don't covet. Don't bear false witness. Don't steal. Don't commit adultery. Don't murder. Honor your parents. Don't swear falsely. Don't make idols. Acknowledge that God exists. The only one that is clearly a ritual commandment, one you could say is particular to the Jewish people, is the commandment to honor the Sabbath. Other people have the concept of Sabbath, to be sure, but this commandment tells *us, particularly,* to observe the Sabbath on the seventh day, to cease from most kinds of work, and to praise God. We would not find fault with a non-Jew for failing to observe the Sabbath. It is a commandment specifically related to being a good Jew, not necessarily related to being a good person. All the rest are, in the main, good-person laws. You *would* judge a non-Jew for adultery or murder – these are, in our minds, prohibitions founded on universal laws.

One might argue about two other commandments, namely, "I am the Lord your God" and "You shall not worship idols." One could argue that these are specific to the Jewish people, not anyone else. But it could be argued back that actually, we *do* expect of all people that they somehow acknowledge a Godliness in the world, regardless of how they define it – and that they not think that God is something over which they have power, like an idol. Still, even if you agree that these two commandments are not quite ethical/moral commandments, neither are they exactly ritual ones. So, at worst, you still would have seven of the ten commandments clearly being addressed to all people. They are about being good people, which is *part* of the whole picture of being a good Jew, but is *not* the whole picture.

This week's Torah portion comes to remind us that our covenant demands of us not only that we be good people, but also that we make an effort to do so in this *particular* way we call Jewish.

We liberal Jews have generally been much more responsive to

the universal call to be good people than to the particular call to be responsible Jews.

Our reform movement was born out of the need to say that our tradition had gotten *too* ritualistic and *too* cumbersome. It wanted to say that much of *halacha*, the traditional Jewish law, had become a burden, had failed to evolve historically, in a way that was meaningful to the modern person. It wanted to respond to the reality that we Jews were no longer living in ghettos, or *shtetls*, and in fact now were full-fledged citizens of our host countries. For the first time, we did not live in totally Jewish communities, bound by Jewish laws both in the court and in the home. We were free to interact with other communities as part of the modern world. We were free to consider the scientific notion that much of other ritual law developed through custom, in the realm of human beings, rather than being commanded to us directly by God. As we began to grapple with these new realities, liberal Jews began to ask the following kinds of questions. Must we be bound by ritual laws that do not resonate within us, that do not seem meaningful? Must we keep kosher? Must we follow strictly the laws of Shabbat? Must we keep all the rituals related to mourning a death?

And the answer came: We do not need to feel bound to those ritual laws for the traditional reasons. We are not compelled to follow all the ritual laws because, God said, in the words of the Torah, or the Talmud or the Rabbis, to follow them. "Because I said so" became a little-respected reason to follow the laws. So did "Because this is the way it's always been done." So did: "You don't have the right to question this."

We found that we did have the right to question, and since we were no longer living in totally Jewish communities, communities in which there was an authority that would consider breaking Jewish law the same as breaking any law, and could censure that behavior, we began to look at ritual laws quite differently.

The early Reform Jews gloried in their new-found freedom to question tradition and to decide whether or not it had meaning for the modern-day Jew. In the last fifteen years, liberal Jews have come to many different conclusions about whether a particular law was meaningful. But through all their deliberations, the question they asked was: Is this law important to me *as a Jew*? Not as a human being. They knew that the moral/ethical laws that were incumbent on all human beings were necessarily part of being a good Jew, but they *also* knew, and never seemed to doubt, that those more ritual laws were incumbent upon us as Jews, too. They were laws that were addressed only to this particular purpose; they were critical principles that ought to have the force of law behind them.

Now, we have forgotten. Most of us have just forgotten. And we have come to see Jewish ritual law not as something we are allowed to question and reject if it seems to have lost its meaning, but as a quaint set of customs we might participate in if we feel like it and happen to be free that day. We have neglected the part of our covenant that says you were called to be *Jews*, not just good people; and if you do not do particular, ritual kinds of things, you will lose that Jewishness and the mind-set, the framework, of Jewish life will be quite lost to liberal Jews.

We need to face the complicated question of what we ought to do, ritually, as Jews. This covenant, in the Torah portion for the Shabbat during *Pesach,* makes a number of ritual demands on us. Among them is the commandment to observe the three main festivals of Jewish life: *Succot, Pesach* and *Shavuot.* Each festival is brimming with meaning. We cannot dismiss them by saying they are without modern-day value.

Wrestling With Ritual

And by and large we don't. Most of us will have participated in at least one Seder this year. Many of us acknowledge *Succot* by participating in building a *succah* at the Temple and saying the appropriate blessings. Fewer of us make it a point to join together for our *Shavuot* observance – its rituals are less compelling, even though their meaning undoubtedly does speak to us today. So, one way or another, our community as a whole still manages to observe the essence of these festivals, even if each one of us does not do so individually.

While we do not dismiss these festivals, however, neither do we take the time or expend the energy to educate ourselves as to the content and meaning of each of these rituals, and then *choose*, actively, not passively, which rituals we feel it is incumbent upon us to keep. That is what the early Reform Jews had in mind. They did not mean for traditions to slip away, unnoticed. They meant for them to be learned and understood and *then* either carefully rejected, for good reason, or lovingly embraced as a necessary part of our religious life.

Case in point: Each of these festivals requires, as part of its observance, a *Yizkor* service – on the eighth day of *Succot*, the seventh day of *Pesach*, and the second day of *Shavuo*t. Each is considered a holiday, like the Sabbath. No work is to be done on those days and each person is commanded, positively, to share in communal prayer at the synagogue. Part of that prayer is a memorial service, a brief section of psalms and readings, including the traditional mourning prayers *El Molei Rachamin* and *Kaddish*. In gatherings that are small enough, each person, or the Rabbi, calls the names of the people for whom the participants regularly say Kaddish throughout the year. If you have lost an immediate relative – mother, father, sister, brother, husband/wife, son, daughters – that person's name ought to be called out loud at *Yizkor* service on *Succcot, Pesach* and *Shavuot*.

Leaning on God

Each of those festivals brings us great joy; we celebrate abundance at *Succot*, freedom at *Pesach*, the giving of the Torah at *Shavuot*. Each is a time of family celebration, of increased awareness of life. With such awareness comes the equal and opposite awareness of loss, of all that we do not have, of all those who are not here, of all the sadness and pain since the last festival. The tradition teaches that opposite side must be expressed as well. Whenever we celebrate, we cheat ourselves if we do not somehow acknowledge that part of us which is not joyful. That part is always there, just as there are always some members of our community, on any given holiday, who are feeling the pain and sadness of life, much more than they can feel the joy, just because of the circumstances of their lives. For them, *Yizkor* is comforting. For all of us, *Yizkor* is helpful. It gives a balance and forces us to experience the wholeness of life, not just a part of it.

Did we liberal Jews stop gathering for festival *Yizkor* services because we found them not to be meaningful? More likely, because no one ever explained to us what they were for. Or fewer and fewer people started showing up, so they became less meaningful and kind of dull. Or we got too busy and it was too much to ask of us to take additional days off. Or we did not like thinking about life and death, so we did not come. Some probably really *did* consider the meaning of *Yizkor* and found that it did not speak to them, and so rejected this ritual. Some of us are just so unused to having religious rituals in our lives and so uninterested in them, that it would not occur to us to consider a *Yizkor* service.

I want to suggest that participating in this ritual may be meaningful. And we would be truer to the covenant we have with God as *Jews* if we give it some thought, rather than not noticing it or rejecting it out of hand. You still might not be interested in *Yizkor*

Wrestling With Ritual

services – but you would be a better Jew for having thought about it. Give it some thought. It is that process and not what we ultimately decide to do, that makes us responsible Reform Jews, that ties ritual to covenant, the essence of being a Jew.

A RABBINIC COMMUNITY CHANGES
(1989)

Last week, I attended Shabbat services at the Plum Street Temple in Cincinnati, Ohio. It was a remarkable experience. Just over seven hundred Reform rabbis had made the journey to this birthplace of America Reform Judaism, to celebrate one hundred years of the official organization of Reform rabbis, the Central Conference of American Rabbis.

When Isaac Mayer Wise created the CCAR a century ago, he had something in mind that was quite different from what the CCAR has turned out to be. He saw the organization as a kind of *Sanhedrin*, a place where liberal rabbis would set standards for themselves, where Jewish legal boundaries would be agreed on and enforced. The CCAR has developed to be both much less and much more. It is less in that the Conference has chosen to be a place of scholarship, debate, and discussion rather than a place of legal decision-making. The CCAR votes on resolutions on subjects as varied as a new response to Soviet Jewry, or day care in Jewish institutions, or responses to actions taken on the West Bank, or whether it is crucial for all Jewish festivals to be observed on their original Hebrew date. But the CCAR has no power to coerce. The Conference as a whole does not dictate positions or take action against individuals who deviate from the majority position.

So if the Conference is not a legal body in the way Isaac Mayer Wise had envisioned, what is it? It is much, much more. The CCAR is a community. It is almost an extended family. It is a support group for those people who have staked their lives on the ultimate value of liberal Jewish life, and who spend their time struggling to understand how best to live in consonance with Jewish values, in our complicated, twentieth century world. The members meet once a year to study, to think, to be refreshed by the company of others who are struggling with similar issues. The Conference publishes a journal to encourage scholarship, it provides placement services, it supports retired or disabled rabbis who are unable to support themselves, it passes resolutions to ensure lively and articulate interactions between Rabbis and the important issues of the day. The Central Conference of American Rabbis is a community, in much the same way a synagogue is a community. It is a synagogue of Rabbis who have the wisdom to know that they need one another, just as the members of any synagogue need one another.

So this community, over half of whose members were present at this year's conference, had the opportunity to do the thing that binds any Jewish community together: we prayed together. In a very lovely return to a taste of an earlier time, we 700 Rabbis were all lodged within easy walking distance of the Plum Street Temple. As the sun set, we found ourselves meeting one another in the street as we walked to Shabbat services, slowly descending on the synagogue, until, almost unnoticed, we had filled it to capacity and were gathered in the strength of our numbers to welcome the Sabbath Bride.

The Plum Street Temple was an auspicious place for this gathering. The Temple was built in 1866, and it reflects the style of Classical Reform Judaism. It is awesome, and it is meant to be awesome. The Temple was designed in the Moorish style of large, elaborate facades, soaring ceilings engraved with intricate designs, elegant wooden pews covered with luxurious velvet fabrics. This was no *shul*; it was a synagogue. It was intended to inspire; to silence. It was created for orderly, respectful, early American Reform Jewish worship, in which the congregation sat politely, in stillness, while a polished minister preached and an angelic choir sang songs that were much too complex for congregational participation, but so beautiful. This was a building of early Reform Jews, who had struggled so hard to move away from the tone of Eastern European Jewishness, and to move into the modern world of enlightened culture. This is the world of Reform Judaism that valued social justice and an ethical society above all else.

Worship there last Friday night was both beautiful and frustrating. The service was a compilation of prayers from all the prayer books used in Reform Judaism, from its birth, until the publication of the current prayer book, *The Gates of Prayer*. It was full of images of an unreachable God, entirely beyond us; it used, almost exclusively, masculine language and formal pronouns, as in: "As Thou hast redeemed Israel, and saved him from arms stronger than his own" and "Rejoice, heaven and earth, be glad that He cometh, be glad for He cometh to judge the earth, He will judge the earth in righteousness." It even excerpted one prayer, the *Kedusha*, from the earliest Reform book, in its original German, and we found ourselves praying, or trying to, in others' language that has many complicated associations for us. The service was meant to be a retrospective on the growth and development of American Reform Judaism. And, although it had some beautiful moments, not a few of which drew their power from the fact that the words and music were reminiscent of our childhoods, the service was, ultimately, a failure. As much as we appreciate our past, it was so very clear that we have grown beyond it. There will be no more silent reserved worshippers in Reform congregations listening to hidden, angelic choirs. We have grown so secure in our identities as Americans, and as twentieth century modern people, that we are able now to return to the communal forms of prayer we knew from our past. We can sing and pray together, with emphasis more on participation than on pure beauty, drawing strength from the rituals of our people's past.

Friday night, we looked back on our past with deep appreciation, but we were not moved by our prayer. Saturday morning, we clearly made a leap into the second hundred years of our existence as an organization, with a service compiled by Rabbi Chaim Stern, editor of our *Gates of Prayer*, in which he moved beyond the gates of prayer to a service informal in style, including much traditional chanting, numerous images of God and beautifully written God language that gently rejected the traditional image of a masculine God acting as Lord and Father.

We sang in unison. We studied the Torah portion, reading from *Chumashim*, Bibles, in our own hands, as the portion was chanted from the *bima*. We were not a passive audience. We were an active community, praying and studying. We felt God's presence among us. We left with a new hope for the possibility of prayer, which I bring back to you this Shabbat.

And we learned, Shabbat morning, from the Rabbi *par excellence*, Rabbi Jacob Rader Marcus. Born in 1896, Rabbi Marcus just celebrated his 93rd birthday. Jacob Rader Marcus joined the faculty of the Hebrew Union College in 1920, and ever since he has been training Reform Rabbis about the history of American Judaism (a field he single-handedly made a respected academic discipline) and, more importantly, the fine art of *menschlekeit*. Rabbi Marcus, in good health but finally beginning to feel his age, leaned on the arm of a newly-ordained student as he walked to and from the podium. But while he stood at that podium, and spoke to so many who had been his students, he drew strength from some inner resource and became completely animated, full of life, energy and vigor.

Jacob Marcus spoke of many things: of his early days teaching at the college; of surviving the unfolding facts of the Holocaust, until its full reality was revealed; of responding to the birth of the state of Israel; of marrying, naming, and burying so many of his students, his colleagues, their children and grandchildren. He spoke with a grand sweep of experience that few of us will ever know. And he made two profound statements, which will ring clearly in my mind for a very long time.

After humbly greeting all the many of his students and teachers assembled there and, in a disarming way, noting the difficulty of saying something worthy of them, he stared us down, each one of us, and said: "You are my legacy."

All of us, generations of his students, were what he had to bequeath to this world, the only thing of value and importance.

A Rabbinic Community Changes

It was clear that all he had learned and taught in his lifetime was preserved in us, that his wisdom would not die with him. "You are my legacy." And we understood the message: do not let it die with you; find students and teach them. And so his message applies to all of you. Your wisdom, what you have understood about living in this world, why we do it and how we do it, this is your real legacy. Do not let it die with you. Find students, students of life, and talk with them, about the things that matter. Leave your legacy of wisdom, through people.

And second, Jacob Rader Marcus said, as he summed up his life's experiences: "the true *nechama*, which means consolation, the true *nechama*, the true comfort, is to face reality."

And you knew this was a man who spoke from experience. In 93 years of living he had faced it all.

"The true *nechama* is facing reality." The Hebrew word *nechama* is so important, because it also has been chosen as the name of the organization in our community that is responding to those among us with AIDS. *Nechama* – consolation. In them, and for us, the only consolation, will come from facing reality.

It is true for so many other issues in our lives, both public and private: Israel, nuclear war, the environment, assimilation, death, divorce, loss of any kind; from change in our lives, which usually forces us to grow, in painful ways, to not enough change in our lives, which prevents our growth, in painful ways. Simple words from our elder: the true *nechama* is to face reality.

One left the presence of Jacob Rader Marcus with a sure knowledge that Reform Judaism was alive and well. Indeed, one left this entire convention quite inspired. From the origins of the movement, as signified by our locale, to the participation in this wisdom of Rabbi

Leaning on God

Marcus, we felt that we were part of history, a history which all of us Rabbis now strive to bring to you. We look back in celebration and forward in inspiration, and we know that we are part of something transcendent.

HOMOSEXUALITY AND JUDAISM
(1990)*

The words we use to bless this *Rosh Hashanah* day move me deeply. They reverberate through my being and fill my soul with hope and compassion. We pray: "May this day add meaning to our lives. Let the Shofar's sound awaken the voice of conscience, our common worship unite us in love, our memories of bondage impel us to help the oppressed."

These words ask us to rise to the highest level possible. This day we are not satisfied with getting by; we challenge ourselves to look for deeper levels of meaning. This day we do not let matters slip by

---

* Adapted, in part, from a sermon by Rabbi Margaret Holub. Reprinted with permission from Rabbi Holub.

unquestioned; we allow the call of the shofar to re-activate the voice of conscience. This day we do not allow ourselves to focus on one another's faults and inadequacies; we focus on the bonds that hold us together as a community, and we gaze upon one another with a Godly sense of acceptance and love of the other. This day we do not allow our complacency to distance us from the pain of others who are still oppressed; we draw on our own experience of oppression to reach out to them with tender care.

So this is the day we can speak together of a difficult and complex subject, one which will call upon us to use these High Holy Day skills and attitudes: searching for meaning; listening for the voice of conscience; accepting one another with love; and responding to the needs of the oppressed.

Many of you know that this year's meeting of the Central Conference of American Rabbis was historic. The Conference adopted in full a report from the Ad Hoc Committee on Homosexuality and the Rabbinate, and passed, by a vast majority, a resolution stating that all rabbis, regardless of sexual orientation, be accorded the right to be ordained, and thereby have the opportunity to fulfill the sacred vocation they have chosen. This decision came after four years of intense study and struggle. Since 1977, the Conference has been on record as supporting vigorously all efforts to eliminate discrimination against gays and lesbians in housing and employment. And, during these years of study, the CCAR, together with the UAHC, the organization of Reform Jewish congregations of which our synagogue is a member, called upon rabbis and congregations to treat all Jews, regardless of sexual orientation, with respect and to integrate them fully into the life of the community. As the resolution affirming the right to ordination passed the Conference this year, there was an immediate burst of applause which turned into a standing ovation of several minutes' duration. On that day, I was proud to be a member of the Conference.

On *this* day of new beginnings and new hopes, I put before you a resolution that goes further than the resolution adopted by the Conference, the affirmation of which I have arrived at after twelve years of journeying through the issues related to Judaism and homosexuality.

I believe that it is just as good, just as moral, just as worthy to be gay or lesbian as it is to be heterosexual. More than that, I believe that any less that this statement is homophobia – fear of homosexuality and bigotry against homosexuals.

As I say this, I am more than aware that many of you have your own strongly-felt positions on this issue, and that they may be quite different from the point of view you will hear from this *bima* today. So I begin by reiterating two of the values we've already spoken of – that we are here this *Rosh Hashanah* morning in a search for meaning, not controversy, and that we are called today to accept one another in love, valuing the other's personhood, and hearing what each has to say in openness, understanding it as a reflection of his or her own life experiences. As I expect you to be open-minded and fair as you listen to what I have to say today, so I affirm your right to come to different conclusions. The words I will speak are, as always, my understanding of what Judaism calls us to do, what God wants of us, as filtered through my study and my understanding of the world. I place them before you for your consideration.

In the twelve years since I began rabbinic school, I have come to know many homosexual people. Most of them were studying to become rabbis or cantors, or were active members of congregations with which I worked. I found myself curious about them, and always asking the judgmental question, "Is this all right, or isn't it?" The more I got to know these people, of course, the more they became people to me, not homosexual people. And when it became time to consider the question of the ordination of gay and lesbian Jews as rabbis, my strongest response came on the personal level: How could so-and-so, whom I know to be an excellent rabbi, a learned and moral person, a thoughtful and committed Jew, not be permitted rabbinic ordination? How could it be that the urge to mate with a person of one's own sex could mitigate all that?

As I was growing up, I learned stereotypes about homosexuals: they are different from us, they are promiscuous, they don't create family bonds, they are obsessed by sexual matters, and by their very nature, they live on the fringes of society.

Now my very good friend who grew up in West Texas learned that Jews have horns, they are stingy (even though they own all the banks and radio and TV stations), they are descendants of the murderers of Jesus and condemned to damnation because they still, arrogantly and stubbornly, refuse to believe that Jesus was the son of God.

Homophobia is remarkably similar to antisemitism. It is based on stereotypes, misinformation, and most of all, on lack of personal contact and experience. As such, homophobia is no better than antisemitism. Having ourselves been the victims of oppression, how do *we* become the oppressor? Are we as Jews not called to look deeper than stereotyped attitudes as we struggle to understand what it is to be homosexual?

Two hundred years ago, Moses Mendelssohn said: be a Jew in your home and a man on the street. It was too dangerous, he believed, to flaunt your Jewishness in the larger community, and unnecessary as well. How many of us have thought about homosexuality, "We don't care what goes on in the privacy of people's homes, as long as they don't flaunt it in front of us?" Is speaking of our Judaism in public flaunting our religion? Is mentioning the name of the person you love flaunting your sexuality? Or kissing that person *Shabbat Shalom* at the end of Services? How hard it would be to have to repress in public all our thoughts and feelings about our Jewishness. Countless times more painful, then, to keep the identity of the one you love a secret. Magnify a hundred times any concern you have had about a public Jewish identity, and begin to know what it must feel like to be homosexual in a heterosexual world.

Every gay person has a whole litany of painful rejections in his or her memories, and fears real consequences of a public homosexual identity: job loss, eviction, disinheritance, loss of child custody, banishment from the family, expulsion from school or professional associations, friendships summarily ended, cold shoulders from neighbors, distraught grandparents, all kinds of awkward and embarrassing silences. Often, therefore, there is an enforced secrecy, and this "life in the closet" hurts people. When we participate in it, by being silent, by being unable to openly accept gay and lesbian people, by failing to make it known that they are welcome in our lives, our homes and our synagogues, we become the oppressors, so quickly leaving the memory of our own oppression behind. Like antisemitism, racism and sexism, homophobia is wrong.

As Jews, our struggles with homosexuality seem to fall into three categories.

The first is the textual one. "But doesn't it say in the Torah that homosexuality is a sin?" the discussion might begin. Yes, it does. Leviticus 18 states that a man who lies with a man as he lies with a woman is an abomination before God. Chapter 20 says that such a couple should be put to death. Now, certainly one of the cornerstones of Reform Jewish thought is that we do not take the Torah literally. We would no doubt all agree that certain norms in the Bible, especially sexual norms, are not what we practice, or even what we think appropriate in our own day. There are, for instance, very explicit rules against having sexual contact with a menstruating woman, for a period of nearly two weeks. Called the laws of *niddah*, these continue to be enforced strictly in many forms of Judaism, with a penalty second only to death in severity. As Reform Jews, we are well practiced in being informed by traditional texts, but not unthinkingly ruled by them.

The line of reasoning continues. It's more than just the one text. What about the implied sin of Sodom and Gomorrah, which is part of the overriding sense of normative Judaism that it is wrong to be homosexual? In actuality, however, surprisingly little is said about homosexuality, not even directly in the story of Sodom and Gomorrah. The two one-line texts in Leviticus are about it. Moreover, they are found in a section of the Torah which is clearly aimed at separating Jewish practice from pagan practices. In Chapter 18, the commandment before it reads: "Do not allow any of your offspring to be offered up to Molech," one of the pagan Gods. In Chapter 20: "If any person turns to ghosts and familiar spirits, and goes astray after them, I will set My face against that person, and cut him off from among his people." It may well be that the real concern here was about idolatry, and not about homosexuality at all.

In addition, to my knowledge, there is not a single reference to lesbianism anywhere in our tradition. It is probably fair to say that what *is* said about homosexuality in our texts is overwhelmingly negative, but that it is extremely sparse. And there are other texts equally compelling. Our tradition has taught Jewish leaders to read text broadly, and to read with their hearts. When they needed texts to speak out in support of the civil rights movement, they found them – "for you were strangers in the land of Egypt;" "let justice roll down like waters." They made wise and powerful inferences from our tradition.

The second argument against homosexuality goes something like this: It is critically important for Jews to marry and to have families, so heterosexual, procreative families are held up as our ideal. The problem is that not every Jew is a heterosexual person, who can find an appropriate spouse, who is capable of having a child and is a suitable person to raise that child. We are tremendously varied, we human beings. Some of us are heterosexual; some are homosexual. There is a tremendous pain in being forced to live a life that is not authentic to you. To ask a homosexual person to live in a heterosexual marriage is to force that person to deny who he or she is, and to inflict misery. Heterosexual marriage is a fine ideal for heterosexual people. It is enslavement for homosexual people.

Further, while we encourage parenthood as a natural act of embracing and furthering human life, sadly not every Jew is capable of having a child. Some Jews know themselves to lack what it takes to be a good parent. When these people live in committed, monogamous relationships, do we consider them to be any less as Jews for their not having children? Do we have a right to hold homosexual Jews to a higher standard, by insisting that they are less than fully Jewish if they do not procreate? And, of course, many homosexuals *do* have families and raise children, and their children are some of the most wanted, loved, cared-for children to crawl on the face of the earth.

The third argument goes: It somehow just isn't natural. The linguistic philosopher A. J. Ayer has said: "There really is no discourse in moral discourse." All moral argument eventually gets down to something like "homosexuality – yuck" or "homosexuality – mmm." People say "I just don't like it; it gives me the creeps." There is no answer to that but "Just because you don't like something doesn't mean it's wrong for someone else to do it." But we should look inside ourselves for a minute and see if homosexuality gives us the creeps, provokes such a "yuck" response. Many people feel that way, and often that is the root of their other argumentation.

Why they feel that way is hard to articulate. Let me suggest one reason that people, Jews in this instance, might be anxious about homosexuality. We know that in Leviticus lepers are called *tameh*, unclean, separate, something you can't touch. It's easy to understand. What happens when you touch a leper? People are afraid of infection. We also know that a menstruating woman, or a woman right after childbirth, is also called *tme'ah*. This is a little harder to understand; you can't catch anything from touching a menstruating woman. But most anthropological information about menstrual taboos says that they come from men fearing women. And when we are afraid of things, we want them out of the camp, away where they can't hurt us.

So is it surprising that homosexuality is excoriated by our tradition? Most people, if not every person, feel some attraction to people of their own sex. Many people act on that attraction, more than one in three men according to Kinsey. Given the realities of our world, who wouldn't be afraid to feel a little bit gay? And, by extension, who wouldn't feel afraid of the people who bear witness to the full fruition of what we fear inside ourselves?

But what if we said: Homosexuality may be strange, intimidating, hard to understand. It may make us feel funny things. It may leave us with questions and things we are curious about and things we are embarrassed to talk about. But it is in no way loathsome. It is fine, it is good. And familiarity and conviviality will diminish the strangeness and lessen the fear, as friendliness usually does.

It's all right to have gay rabbis and cantors and gay camp counselors and Temple presidents, gay fundraisers and religious school teachers. And, of course, we do. But they shouldn't be forced into hiding.

Jews and homosexuals share a piece of history. The Nazis were most effective in oppressing both. As they made Jews wear yellow stars, they made homosexuals wear pink triangles and sent more than 50,000 gay men to concentration camps. Last year, Rabbi Alex Schindler, president of the UAHC, noted that there is an interpretation of the Jewish star that any child with a crayon can tell you, that the Star of David contains within it the triangle. For those of us who have been willingly blind to the geometry of Jewish life, who would keep invisible the presence of the triangle within the shield of David, it is time to complete the outline of our Jewish star.

We are a varied people, we human beings. And as we sit in our congregation this *Rosh Hashanah*, we represent the wonderful variety of God's creation. We are singles and families, homosexuals, heterosexuals, black, white, old, young, infertile, and raising children. We are all here; that is a fact. Now, let us all be welcomed, openly and freely; and, as we pray in many of our *Shabbat* Services, let the wanderer come home from exile.

INTERFAITH WEDDINGS
(1997)

This is a Rabbi's nightmare. Here I stand, virtually unknown to most of the rest of the rabbis here at the 1997 gathering of the Pacific Association of Reform Rabbis, and I am about to speak on interfaith weddings, which may well be the most personally highly-charged subject discussed in the Jewish world today. I do not see the faces worn familiar by many *Shabbeses* spent together, endless congregational controversies somehow negotiated and healed, births celebrated and deaths mourned together; instead, I look out at the faces of strangers expectantly waiting to hear their views either defended or denied. We who serve in congregations know that we can use an inapt word or make other mistakes, because there is next week, next month, next year, to hear how our words have been received, to think and re-think an issue along with our people. It is

Interfaith Weddings

strange to me to take these same risks with strangers, as it must be for you to hear words that will challenge you so strongly, or affirm you so completely, from one who is an outsider to the workings of your minds and your hearts.

The situation is further complicated by the passions we bring to the subject. The story of our sister, or daughter, cousin, brother or son, or our own interaction with a Rabbi, who did or did not officiate at the wedding, and the full weight of that act on our family's history, on our own feelings about the rabbinate, and on what it means to be Jewish – all of that is here with us in this room, and realistically threatens to keep us from being truly open and hearing one another.

So I say to you, at the end of this lengthy preamble: I have prepared myself over these last weeks to take the risk, to share with you in as open a fashion as I know how, all that I can grasp about the complicated phenomenon of Jews and non-Jews marrying, and what our Rabbinic part in that ought to be. And so I ask of you to still the voices raging in your minds, for a moment. Let the preconceived ideas and the long-held passions go, and allow yourselves to absorb the words I am about to speak, before you judge what I say.

As I grappled with why it was so difficult for me, originally, to get a handle on what I wanted to say, my husband the lawyer told me it was because of a legal axiom he calls "the sky is blue." One has trouble arguing for that which seems so patently clear and obvious.

To me, it has always been abundantly clear that I, as a Rabbi, ought only to officiate at the wedding of two Jews. In the milieu in which I was raised, a classical reform synagogue, Rabbis simply did not officiate at interfaith weddings. It was not even a hard decision, but was taken for granted. And so it was for me, all through rabbinic school, through my assistantship at Congregation Beth Israel in Houston, Texas, and well into my years here in Southern California. Slowly, though, I found that colleagues whom I admired and respected were changing their minds and beginning to officiate under certain conditions. Yet, while I listened and learned and understood, and heard with greater understanding and passion the comments of interfaith couples who came to me, for me the given remains a given. I understand my role as Rabbi to include the privilege of acting as *mesaderet kiddushin*, the one who organizes the Jewish rituals of marriage, only when it is two Jews who will be coming together to say the ancient words and perform the ritual acts.

I hope to explain this deeply-held conviction by sharing a principle, four reasons, three related issues, a story, a strategy, and a conclusion.

The principle, on which I have based my entire rabbinate and which has brought great meaning to my chosen way of life and, I believe, has brought whatever success I may have achieved in my rabbinate, is that the reality that exists beneath the surface is far more important than whatever events are presenting themselves superficially. In order to bring a sense of holiness and meaning to any ritual moment, one must be grasping and articulating that deeper reality. The rituals of a baby-naming, for instance, take on power when the family dynamics are understood and captured within the ritual. Has the couple had difficulty conceiving? Is this the first grandchild? Did a grandparent die recently? A ritual, powerful in and of itself, that is used to reflect a deeper reality, can fill the aching desire we have for a sense of spirituality that orders our lives. How many Passover Seders have we all attended, or even conducted, that have not moved us because we were somehow unable to get to the meaning behind the words, bring the deeper reality behind the symbols to the surface.

Interfaith Weddings

The words become perfunctory. Although we have a ritual moment, we do not have a taste of holiness.

What I say to interfaith couples that come to me is that, in order for their wedding ceremony to have meaning and integrity, the ceremony must accurately reflect the religious commitments of both partners. If it does not, the couple will be married, but the moment will not have been filled with truth and meaning and holiness. It will have been a perfunctory ritual that, in the end, diminishes, rather than expresses, the holiness of the bond they will create.

So I arrive at the four reasons, which are the reality almost always lying just beneath the surface of an interfaith Jewish wedding ceremony.

1. The non-Jewish partner rarely has internalized the meaning of the symbols, the metaphors, the words of a Jewish wedding. I can teach them, surely, but such things take time and attention to sink in, to develop meaning. Unless a person is actively working at developing a Jewish identity (an enormously difficult task in itself), he or she would not be in a position to fill the words and the actions of the ceremony with meaning. For a non-Jew to say and do Jewish things, as an outsider looking in, borrowing that tradition, trying it on, offering it as an act of love to one's beloved, is to diminish the power and the veracity of those rituals, no matter how sincere the intention. The words and actions on the surface do not match the reality beneath, and the ceremony has a false ring to it; it loses integrity. Similarly, a non-Jew in such a situation may agree to raise a child as a Jew, but what really can that mean? How much can a person who has not committed himself or herself to living as a Jew in this world pass on Jewish meaning to a child? I acknowledge that there are exceptions to the rule; I have seen them. But most often, the words: "I agree to raising the children Jewish," means something like:

"I will not get in the way of my spouse's raising the children Jewish, if he/she is moved to do so."

2. There are a great many situations in which the Jewish ceremony is desired, in the main, to keep someone else happy, a parent or a grandparent, but in no way reflects the commitments of the couple. This is nice; it may keep people happy. But it is not good or honest. It is not real. It will not create a sense of holiness. It is not the job of a Rabbi.

3. In most situations, there is a high probability that there is some sort of coercion of the non-Jewish partner going on, at however subtle a level.

4. There is some sense of the Rabbi's colluding with the bride and groom, to create a reality for the extended family and friends and for the couple that is simply not true. By his or her presence, the Rabbi suggests that this problem is somehow solved, that we can smooth over the conflict in an interfaith relationship by creating together a beautiful, and seamless wedding ceremony, in which everyone pretends that there is no disagreement. But there *is* disagreement, and it usually does not take too long to surface and, often, to explode.

The integrity, the meaning, the power of *kiddushin*, a Jewish wedding ritual, is completely undermined by the presence of any or all of those realities. A marriage takes place; a deeply meaningful, holy moment does not. Jewish ritual has been used for other than its rightful purpose.

What I tell a couple that comes to me is that their marriage is much more important than the wedding ceremony that will unite their lives. Their *marriage*, what kind of religious life they can have together, how, in honesty, should they raise their children together, are the questions crying out for their attention. Some couples can deal with these in a

Interfaith Weddings

straightforward way before the planned wedding, and that often results in a conversion. Many know they cannot, and I urge them to have a civil ceremony, perhaps bringing to it elements of each of their traditions, bringing to the surface the conflicts, and committing themselves to resolving those conflicts in some meaningful way, over time. The wedding ceremony must reflect the current religious convictions of the bride and groom, in order for it to have integrity and meaning.

Three related issues:

1. I do my best to communicate to the couple that, in each other, they may have found the ideal life partner. I understand that, and as a person, I rejoice with them. But as a Rabbi, as a symbol of Jewish life, I cannot fully rejoice with them, because for the Jewish people, it is not the ideal choice.

2. We live in a world that teaches us that our choice of life partner is a purely personal one. I represent a tradition that teaches it is a communal, as well as a personal one. The Jewish community has a stake in Jews choosing Jewish partners, and must be saddened by the risks involved in Jews choosing otherwise. In this way, I can affirm them, welcoming them to my synagogue, while not officiating at the ceremony, without any inconsistency.

3. And welcome them I do, with overwhelming warmth. They receive, for instance, the same first year's membership as any other new member, as a gift from the congregation. They receive the insistent continuing invitations that they join a *chavurah*, and come to a study session with me as often as possible. For all the reasons we are trying hard to understand, the Jewish partner's Judaism was not compelling enough, not enough at the core of his or her being, to motivate the choice of a Jewish partner. Now I see it as my task to communicate to both of them the possibility of a Judaism that *is* compelling.

Leaning on God

The story: They were married by a Rabbi unconnected to the synagogue before I came to the congregation. He was Jewish, raised in the congregation; his parents are still members. She was Catholic and they loved each other very much. The groom and the parents desperately wanted a Jewish wedding and they got one. The couple agreed to raise any children Jewish. They had terrible trouble conceiving, and when a child was finally born, the wife came to see me. She said: "When we were trying so hard to have a baby I prayed to Jesus, and swore that I would dedicate my child to Christ if I ever was blessed with one. I have to have my baby baptized. I'm sorry, I'm sorry," she cried. "I've broken my promise."

Is it the officiation that mattered? Probably not. Could some insightful, serious counseling at the time of the wedding have helped? Maybe. This situation can only truly be mitigated in the future by a new commitment to living and teaching all that it means to be a Jew, and by re-creating a Judaism that is not peripheral to our people's lives, but is at their core.

This, then, is the strategy.

I worry and wonder about what I will do, if he chooses to marry a non-Jew. I can feel the sorrow already, standing side by side with my joy, if he has otherwise chosen well for himself. I know I would not want to see him married in a Jewish ceremony. We are a realistic and truthful people. For whatever complicated reasons, his Jewishness would not have been enough at his core, to determine his choice. If there is a *chuppa* and breaking of the glass, is there any less truth that my son is married to a non-Jew and the future of Judaism in their love is at risk?

I love my son more than my God. If I were Abraham, I would have failed the test; I would not have delivered him up as a sacrifice. So I will accept, and – pray God – eventually love, the daughter-in-law with

Interfaith Weddings

whom I am presented, but I would not prevaricate, confuse, make do, make believe, by pretending that what is there is not, for the pleasure of seeing my son married in the way I always envisioned it, for the hope that a Jewish ceremony could urge them toward a more Jewish life.

My son Joe is almost four years old. My husband and I are currently engaged in a lively debate about day school versus public school. I want him to go to a day school. I want Jewish values and Jewish rhythms to form the core of his life now, because I know they will be so encroached upon later. That is the nature of life in a society as open as the one we are blessed to live in. Yet we are so liberal as to still care deeply about the public school system and are unhappy at the idea of abandoning it.

So, if it comes to an intermarriage in my own family, and I must acknowledge that it could, I see myself only choosing to make Judaism always and ever open to this new family, showing them, welcoming them, over and over again, helping them come to terms with their conflicts, honestly, in a way that is meaningful to them, as I am compelled to do with any interfaith couple I know.

The conclusion: I feel that I must say a word about the more particular issue you will be voting on in the resolution to be discussed this evening.

I have not been in job placement for some time, but when I last was, more than ten years ago, I knew I lost one congregation because I was female and one because I did not officiate at interfaith weddings.

The task of a Rabbi is to think this matter through, carefully and seriously. A Rabbi ought not to be judged by his or her stance on this issue (not to mention by his/her gender), but by the quality of the thought process behind it, and by the integrity with which he or she lives out decisions carefully made.

Leaning on God

When a majority of Rabbis feel so strongly about an issue, even one as complex as this, it is nothing less than critical for them to take a public stand on the matter. We need not diminish or handicap, and certainly not punish, colleagues among us who conclude otherwise. They are part of the great diversity of our movement. If anything, this autonomy is what our movement stands for. But our great tolerance for diversity must not keep us from what a great majority of us stand for, what we believe in even as we hold higher the value of the right of particular members to believe and act otherwise. We are called upon to be the leaders, the visionaries. Part of that is setting boundaries for the community as best as we can.

How can we possibly have any integrity as a Rabbinic organization if we do not? If we do not state clearly the things in which we believe? Even if many Rabbis among us draw the boundary elsewhere. So be it. Let us continue to engage in fruitful dialogue. Let our ideas be tested in debate.

My writer friend gave me the gift of this line from William Butler Yeats. "Man can embody the truth, but he cannot know it." It may be that none of us ever can know the absolute truth of this matter, whether it is best, objectively, to officiate or not. We can only know the truth that resonates in our own souls, and pray that we each find the courage to act that truth out, with integrity, in our Rabbinates, because of what we believe, most deeply.

I conclude, finally, with my own quote, the words I pray each time I carry a sheaf of yellow papers like this to a podium.

Yihyu L'ratzon imrafei, v'hegyon libi, lefanecha

May the words that come forth from my mouth, and the innermost thoughts of my heart, be pleasing before you.

Adonai Tsuri, v'goali.

Interfaith Weddings

O my God, my Rock, the one who supports me, the only one who can redeem me, may my words reflect your presence. May they have served you well.

May each of us come to a conclusion in our thoughts about this matter that we believe serves God, our Rock and our Redeemer, serves God well.

LANGUAGE AND THE PAST

December 30th, 1983. Only one more day to cross off in the datebook, only one more page to tear off the calendar and it will be here. 1984. The much awaited, much discussed, almost legendary 1984. 1984 – the symbol of the far-away future, of a time when we will have allowed our society's technological advances and desire for power to destroy all that we now hold dear and precious. Can it be, we wonder, that 1984 is actually here?

Or do we? Frankly, it seems to me that the mythical element of the very phrase 1984 is diminishing, rather than growing, the closer we approach the proverbial date. We've already bought our 1984 calendars and penciled in appointments for various dates during the year. We know this is the '83-'84 school year. We talk easily about the '84 elections. 1984? Well, it's not really affecting us more deeply than any other new year. 1984 – surprisingly enough, it feels almost normal.

Language and the Past

And yet, the newspapers and magazines and talk shows are all asking the question: Is this year 1984 going to fulfill the prophecies made by George Orwell in his novel *1984*, written more than 35 years ago? Are we becoming controlled by our technology? Are we embarked on a path toward a totalitarian, brutal, repressive world in which human freedom and dignity are unknown? Are we approaching a time when each individual human person is completely powerless, not only to act, but even to think private thoughts?

Is Big Brother, the ever-present symbol of the controlling power, always watching us?

In the past few weeks, I've read numerous articles that assess the value of Orwell's book by measuring his terrifying vision of the future against the realities of our world. They ask: Is Orwell's vision actually coming to be? More often than not, these authors dismiss Orwell's *1984* as a science fiction fantasy which, happily, bears little resemblance to the world we are living in. They say that the book fails as a prophecy because it has succeeded as a warning. Confronted with the possibility of a world based on war, hate, and the absolute control of power, we have determined that we will create another path. The notion that *our* 1984 resembles *Orwell's 1984* is pridefully rejected.

And in fact, all these columnists and editorializers are quite correct. One can safely say that Orwell's nightmare has not become our reality. That is why all the talking about the arrival of the year of doom, 1984, seems like nothing more than the proverbial tempest in a teapot. That's why all the articles and discussions are actually kind of boring – everyone's on the same side of the argument.

As I re-read *1984* myself during the past few weeks, I came to this conclusion: all the essayists and columnists and talk show hosts are taking Orwell too literally. They are painting the issue in black and white terms, and as usual, it is just not that simple.

No, our world certainly does not resemble the horror that Orwell created. But have we truly been warned, have we taken sufficient notice, of some of the subtler principles Orwell's society was based on? Have we considered how we will control the development of those principles in our world?

In the preface to a new edition of *1984*, Walter Cronkite observed the following:

> What Orwell had done was not to *foresee* the future, but to see the implications of the present. . . . *1984* is an anguished lament and a warning that vibrates powerfully when we may not be strong enough nor wise enough nor moral enough to cope with the kind of power we have learned to amass.[*]

If there *are* trends in our society that could lead us to an Orwellian world, where *will* we look to find the strength, the wisdom, the morality to control them?

As a Jew, I turn to my tradition regularly, to create order out of chaos, to maintain sanity in the face of craziness, to produce strength when there is no apparent source of strength in the world.

As I re-read *1984* and understood the principles underlying Orwell's society, I understood just as quickly that there exists within the very structure of Jewish life that which refutes a value system that could lead us to an Orwellian 1984. If we live as Jews, we will find

---

[*] Orwell, George. *1984*. Preface by Walter Cronkite. New York: New American Library, 1983 (emphasis in original).

Language and the Past

that we *are* strong enough, wise enough, and moral enough to cope with whatever the modern world forces upon us.

Orwell creates two main concepts for his new world society, Newspeak and Doublethink. While both concepts seem completely outlandish at first, they are also somehow familiar. We are not untouched by the possibilities implied by them.

Newspeak is a special language being developed by the ruling government in *1984*. It was eventually to replace Oldspeak, or standard English. Its purpose was to create a reality in which the only thoughts or concepts that could be expressed in words were those that reflected the ruling power's world view and belief system. This goal was achieved in several ways.

First, any word which expressed an unorthodox or heretical thought was eliminated from the vocabulary. Words such as honor, justice, morality, democracy, science, and religion simply ceased to exist.

Second, undesirable words which could not be completely eliminated were stripped of all secondary meaning. For instance, the word "free" still existed in Newspeak, but it could only be used in such statements as "This field is free from weeds." It could not be used in its old sense of "politically free" or "intellectually free," since political and intellectual freedom no longer existed even as concepts, and therefore were nameless.

Third, thousands of words which expressed ambiguities or shades of meaning were eliminated from the vocabulary and replaced with short words of unmistakable meaning, which roused the minimum of echoes in the speaker's mind. The use of prefixes and suffixes eliminated the need for many words. For instance, "uncold" meant "warm" – "plus cold" meant "very warm" – "double plus cold" meant "superlatively warm." Given the word "good" there was no need for the word "bad;" "ungood" functioned just as well.

Finally, compound words were created to express the world in terms of the orthodox thought of the government in a brief, direct manner. "Good-think" meant "to think in an orthodox manner." "Old-think" meant any idea that was popular before the present government took control, and always implied a sense of wickedness. One character in the book explains: "Don't you see that the whole aim of Newspeak is to narrow the range of thought? In the end, we shall make thoughtcrime literally impossible because there will be no words in which to express it."

Orwell reminds us of a very basic truth. Only that which we have words for, only that which we can at least attempt to articulate, is real for us. What cannot be thought cannot exist. Newspeak was fundamental to Orwell's new society because it completely controlled what it was possible to think.

We understand that language is central to one's view; Jewish language and vocabulary are fundamental to our perspective on the world as Jews. Jewish talk gives us the words to create concepts that otherwise would be unnameable. That which is unnameable does not exist. Judaism provides us with a system that struggles to bring into existence the very concepts Newspeak attempted to eliminate – holiness, godliness, humanity, dignity.

Unlike Newspeak, Jewish vocabulary attempts to communicate worlds of meaning in individual words. Newspeak strives for words with a *minimum* of echoes and associations behind them; as Jews we *search* for the echoes behind our words and those echoes reverberate through our beings, giving us the power to create a world based on values that are articulated and understood.

Language and the Past

Take the Hebrew word *Kadosh*. You may not be familiar with the word out of context, but its basic meaning is "holy." That one word, that one concept describes so many aspects of our lives as Jews. *Kadosh* is the root of the word *Kiddush*, the blessing we say over wine. Wine, our symbol of joy and thankfulness. Wine, which we share at every memorable occasion, acknowledging God as its creator and acknowledging our own ability to take the most mundane, secular act and raise it to a level of Holiness. *Kiddush* – to drink wine – to make holy.

The same root gives us the word *Kaddish*, the prayer by which we memorialize our dead. We say *Kaddish* to remember, to honor, to raise to a level of holiness that which causes our deepest grief. *Kaddish* – to make holy the memory of our dead.

The very same root gives us *Kiddushin* – the Hebrew word for marriage. To enter into a marriage is to enter a state of holiness. The Jewish concept of what marriage should be is communicated in this one special term. It is that bond between two people which raises their relationship to a level of sanctity, which creates holiness to the world through the joining of two souls. Marriage becomes not merely utilitarian or legalistic, but religious, a way of expressing our own striving toward Godliness.

Take the word *mensch*. It's a word that every Jewish person knows. And every Jewish person knows that the highest compliment he or she can receive is to be called a *mensch*. How do we define *mensch*? No one word could ever do it – a person, a person who does the right thing, a person who has strength, character, a person who is truly a human being. Could the concept exist without the word? Perhaps it could, but not with the same power. For Jews, to be a *mensch* is the goal we set before us. *Mensch* is the word that reminds us what we are striving for and what it is possible to become.

Take the word *Shabbat*. It means the seventh day, it means rest, but it means so much more than that. With the word *Shabbat*, Jews have named a concept that raises human life above the rest of the animal world. One word, that insists upon human dignity. One word that says: "You have the right to some peace, to some time. All of your life must not be dominated by work, by action, by the pursuit of things. Some part of your life must be devoted just to being." *Shabbat*, a concept that does not exist without the word.

Jewish language flies in the face of Orwell's *1984*. Newspeak limited life and restricted thought. Jewish language imparts life and creates holiness. If we will use it, keep it alive, and treasure the concepts behind our special words, *1984* can never be.

The other Orwellian concept, Doublethink, allows the human mind to suspend its knowledge of verifiable facts, so that it may accept as true whatever the Party, the ruling government, chooses to call truth. Through Doublethink, any individual could say and believe that 2 + 2 = 5, if the Party chooses to say that that is truth, all the while knowing on some other level that 2 + 2 is not 5, but is 4. The expert at Doublethink actually forgets, temporarily, that 2 + 2 was ever anything but 5.

The main use of Doublethink in *1984* is to control the past. The Party is able to re-write the past any way it chooses in order to prove that the Party always had been correct. It becomes a major task of the government bureaucracy to rewrite newspapers, fabricate pictures, and do whatever else is necessary to prove that the past happened just the way the current ruling party wanted it to have happened.

The main character of the book, Winston Smith, is employed by the government to do the most delicate kinds of fabrication of

Language and the Past

the past. In the final scenes, Winston is being interrogated by the Secret Police and is asked:

> " . . . Does the past exist concretely, in space? Is there somewhere or other a place, a world of solid objects, where the past is still happening?"
>
> [Winston replied] "No!"
>
> "Then where does the past exist, if at all?"
>
> "In records. It is written down."
>
> [The interrogator agrees] "Yes, in records. And—?"
>
> "In the mind," [Winston replies.] "In human memories."
>
> "In memory. Very well then. We, the Party, control all records and we control all memories. Then we control the past, do we not?"
>
> "But how can you stop people remembering things?"*

In the remaining pages of the book, Winston is tortured and brainwashed until he too, finally admits that whatever the Party holds to be truth is truth. And so *1984* makes its final statement. The Party is ultimately and completely in control, and individual human existence is reduced to nothingness. The past is gone. There is no other reality to hold on to but the reality presented by the ruling party.

Judaism, to the contrary, has been obsessed with *preserving* the past. As a people, we are deeply rooted in our history. We constantly remind ourselves who we are and where we have come from.

The center of our tradition is the Torah, which is fundamentally a history book. Each year, as we repeat the cycle of Torah readings, we re-tell the ancient history of our people, communicating our values

---

* Orwell, George. *1984*. New York: New American Library, 1949. p. 205. Print.

and our traditions to the next generation. Our scribes made sure that the Torah text was copied as exactly as possible. The mere fact that our Torah text has remained constant, generation after generation, shows our commitment to preserving for the future our deep connection to our past.

Throughout our prayers, we repeat the historical call to our God, the God of Abraham, Isaac, and Jacob. Each time, we remember that no modern idea, no twentieth-century idol, can take the place of God in our lives. Our God is intrinsically a part of our history as a people. Our understanding of the God of Abraham, Isaac, and Jacob cannot be perverted in any way.

And our cycle of holidays, the festivals we observe year after year, reminds us of our historical link. So many of them are based on a historical occurrence in the life of our people, which gives rise to some ethical or moral value. At Chanukah we re-tell the story of the Maccabees, glorifying their willingness to fight for justice. At *Pesach* we read from our Haggadahs the glorious history of our people's Exodus from Egypt, affirming the right of every person to live in freedom. At *Shavuot*, we remember the wonder of the fact that God created a covenant with the Israelite people at Mt. Sinai, swearing them to keeping the commandments, while promising that the presence of God would never depart from their midst.

As Jews we are dedicated to preserving our history. Always knowing who we are, where we come from and what we value gives us a measure of reality, a standard of truth by which to judge the outside world. Without it we are powerless. With it, even Big Brother would be powerless to confuse us.

Tomorrow, we will all celebrate New Year's Eve. And then January 1, 1984, will arrive. It will not be Orwell's 1984. It will be a year full of potential, in which we will maintain our struggle to create the world the way we want it to be.

May it be a year in which we treasure our history as Jews and live out in our actions the meanings of our holy words, so that we can assure ourselves that Orwell's 1984 will never arrive.

V
GOD

GOD LANGUAGE

Everything in the book of Deuteronomy has sort of a familiar sound to it, like something you have heard before, but you can't quite remember where. The reason this is so is because you probably *have* heard it before. Deuteronomy is Moses' summary of everything that has happened to the people of Israel up to this point, when we are finally at the edge of the Promised Land. The word "Deuteronomy" comes from the Greek, meaning "second law;" it is the second time through, just in case you missed some of it before.

The particular paragraph I read from tonight includes one line that is possibly my favorite in the entire Torah: "God went before them in a pillar of cloud by day to guide them and in a pillar of fire by night." It is that pillar of cloud that interests me the most. There is nothing so distant, yet so obvious as a cloud. There is nothing so elusive, yet so real. The image of the cloud captures something essential about our understanding of God: that God is ever-present, but somehow just out of our reach.

King Solomon shared this fascination with God's presence being symbolized by clouds. Four hundred and eighty years after the Exodus from Egypt, Solomon began the work of building the Temple of the Lord in Jerusalem. When it was completed, clouds filled the sanctuary and Solomon declares: "The Lord has chosen to abide in a thick cloud. I have now built for you a stately house, a place where you may dwell forever."

Feeling a frustration about the *remoteness* of God's presence in the clouds, Solomon builds a Temple, trying to bring God closer. But no sooner has Solomon built the Temple than he himself questions it and, according to the Book of Kings, asks: "But will God really dwell on Earth? Even the heavens to their uttermost reaches cannot contain you, how much less this House that I have built?"

So even King Solomon struggles with the tension between acknowledging that God's presence somehow fills the world, and finding a way to capture it and bring it closer to human life. This struggle does not stop Solomon for long. He turns almost immediately from his philosophical speculation to a much more practical task, asking God for the things he wants. He says: "Yet turn, Oh my God, to the prayer and supplication of your servant and hear the cry and prayer which your servant offers before you this day." Solomon then asks for the following things:

> When one person commits an offense against another and they come for judgment, be sure to condemn he who is in the wrong and reward he who is in the right.

God Language

When the people of Israel are losing in battle because they have sinned against you, accept their repentance and battle for them.

Should the heavens be shut up and there be no rain because they have sinned against you, hear their plea and pardon them and bring rain to your people.

In any plague and in any disease, heal your people Israel.

Solomon has left the cloud imagery behind. He is able to ask God for concrete acts: Be sure that we rule justly; make us win our wars; give us rain; heal our sick. A God who can do such things is no elusive, cloud-type God. These prayers require a God who can hear prayer, and *act* in response to it. So Solomon turns to the more typical images of God we know from the Bible – God as the Master, the King, the Father, the Ruler.

The traditional, Biblical image of God is an anthropomorphic one. A God with human characteristics, capable of answering Solomon's prayers, naturally developed into a God who was stereotypically masculine: the strong, powerful, active King and man of war. Biblical man's natural turning to an image of God as a masculine being made complete sense in the Biblical world. Men fought the wars, planted and reaped the crops, created and enforced a judicial system, and struggled to protect their families from sickness. When they needed help in these tasks, when they prayed for God to intervene in their lives, it only made sense to pray to a God that was like them – strong, active, able to fight wars: Male.

But for me, I find myself much more comfortable with Solomon's cloud image. As twentieth-century people, we seek God's help for a different set of tasks. We find ourselves no longer capable of maintaining faith in an active God who can do the concrete sorts of things Biblical man expected. We *see* the perversion of justice around us every day. Certainly after the Holocaust we no longer can say that the good are rewarded and the evil punished. We see senseless wars being fought, wars in which it is not easy to say which side we think God should favor. We do not see that God actively intervenes to heal the sick, or to bring rain so that the soil will be fertile.

Our needs and our understandings reflect a different world; we come to God with different requests. As a result, we need different language in order to address God, different images to further our understanding. The Biblical image of God as the all-present, all-powerful, masculine warrior and King no longer adequately fulfills our needs for God.

As modern people, we pray for things that are much more abstract than the things Solomon prayed for. We have a need to understand who we are and where we came from, so we appeal to God as the creator. We praise the source of life, but we do not expect that God will intervene actively to save a given individual. We understand God as less of a being and more as a source. We sing praises to the one who supports our doctors and nurses and scientists in their efforts.

We would surely like to understand why the workings of the world sometimes seem to be unjust. While we would like to pray to a superhuman God who could step in and rectify these injustices, we cannot. So we appeal to God for less tangible things, like strength and support. We turn to God in search of comfort, and many times we are able to sense that comfort – not from the Biblical, active God who can change reality, but from a more abstract image of God whose support emanates from the universe.

God Language

As moderns, we cry out to our God that there are people who are starving to death, that poverty abounds, that people perpetrate untold horrors upon one another every day. So we appeal to God as the Redeemer, the one who gives us hope, the one who encourages us to work towards the messianic age.

Using only male language to describe God fosters the notion that God is capable of fulfilling the tasks assigned by Biblical man. And many of us anguish over the fact that we do not believe in such a God. Exclusively male God language worked as a reflection of Biblical man's understanding of the world. It cannot work as a reflection of our world.

This does not imply that there is any need for us to change or revise our holy texts. The Bible stands as a literary unit with integrity. There is no need to purge it of its masculine God; it must simply be understood as a product of the society that created it. The Bible itself must remain in its original form. It is, after all, the only record we have of our ancestors' understanding of the divine.

Our worship services – our present-day responses to God – are, however, ours to create. While the structure of the Jewish worship service is relatively rigid, its language always has been flexible. The words of the traditional service were not even formalized until at least the ninth century, a relatively late date in Jewish history. Our worship service must reflect our understanding of God if it is to create a meaningful experience in our lives. For us to continue to pray solely to the superhuman, masculine image of God will make God less, not more, relevant to our lives.

As I read from the prayer book, I therefore regularly delete masculine references to God, and find some other image to use as a substitute. I do this not because as a woman I am offended or insulted by the image of a male God, but because I find that understanding God in an *exclusively* masculine sense, as our tradition has led us to do, is theologically crippling. Limiting God to the stereotypic masculine role limits the extent to which God can function as a truly meaningful aspect of our lives.

When reading the service, we can change masculine references to God to the neuter. "He" becomes "God;" "Him" becomes "Lord;" "King" becomes "Ruler." The problem with this is that we are robbed of the opportunity to communicate with a personal God. As human beings, we have a desire to talk to someone greater than we, and Judaism has always responded to this need, encouraging the individual to speak to God as a person. On *Yom Kippur* we cry out *Avinu Malkeinu* – Our Father Our King – forgive us, accept our repentance. Tevye the milkman was able to endure his life because he could talk to God, even argue with God, as a friend. We do not want to lose that sense of personal connection with God, yet that becomes a possibility as we begin to address ourselves to a genderless God.

It is possible to approach the issue of God language differently; we can say that there are many useful ways of addressing God, and present a wide variety of the possibilities in our prayers. There are times when we want to pray to an image of God as our Father and our King. Likewise, there may be times when we want to seek out the stereotypically feminine qualities of God. We might want to address God as our Mother, or our Queen. Using feminine terms for God still seems very shocking to us. But that shock illustrates what we often try to deny, that we are deeply committed to our image of God as a male person with male attributes. If that image of God is not fully meaningful to us as modern people, we have both the right and the responsibility to stretch it, to open our minds to other images of

God Language

God: masculine images, feminine images, or any of a wide variety of abstract images suggested to us by our tradition: *El Elyon*, the Most High, *El Olam*, the Everlasting God, *El Shaddai*, Mountainous God, *El Roi*, The One Who Sees.

Developing our God language beyond the purely masculine is not a woman's issue. Admittedly, it is a little peculiar to live in an age when women are fully active and valued in all realms of religious life, and yet not have that activity and value reflected in our understanding of God. But, more importantly, re-examining our ways of talking about and addressing God is a theological issue. A relationship with God is not static; it is not something constant which we can plug into at will. A God language must be developed that will remind us all of what God can be and of the many different ways a sense of Godliness can enter our lives.

A favorite quote of mine from T.S. Eliot comes to mind:

> We shall not cease from exploration.
> And the end of all our exploring
> Will be to arrive where we started
> And know the place for the first time.[*]

The God we are seeking is still the one God of Israel, the God of our ancestors. All of our searching for ways to approach our God will lead us back, finally, to that same known place. But when we say *Shema Yisrael, Adonai Eloheinu, Adonai Echad* – Hear, O Israel, the Lord is our God, the Lord is One – our understanding of that God will be richer for our exploring, and we will truly know our God for the first time.

---

[*] Eliot, T.S. "Little Gidding." *Four Quartets*. New York: Harcourt, Inc., 1971. p 59. Print.

WHAT IT MEANS TO BE CHOSEN

So the Israelite people have gathered together at the foot of Mt. Sinai. They have heard the thunder, they have seen the lightning, they have trembled in their fear and awe. Our tradition teaches that they heard God's voice binding them in a covenant. "I am the Lord your God. You shall have no other Gods before me." They entered into the covenant as they acknowledged God's authority and agreed to do the mitzvah. Thus, the tradition says that, standing at the foot of Mt. Sinai, the Jews became a chosen people. And the tradition goes further: it was not our ancestors alone who stood at Mt. Sinai, but it is just as if we ourselves stood there, in spirit, with them.

They accepted the covenant on our behalf. So not only they but we too became a chosen people.

What It Means to Be Chosen

Jewish tradition affirms that God chose the Jews. To our modern, democratic, rational brains, such a statement often seems absurd, if not offensive. First, many people have trouble accepting an image of God as doing something so specific as *choosing* a particular people, intruding into history in such a direct manner. It is easier for us to understand God's *doing* something more abstractly, as when God causes an inner, personal, human experience, which then produces a new human perspective or action.

Second, we rebel against even the implication that Jews enjoy some special status in the universe, that we have been singled out for some special intimacy with God. We believe in universalism. We believe in the equality of every human person before God. How, then, can we understand the statement that God "chose" the Jewish people?

Let us first understand exactly what the Biblical authors meant when they used this term. In the Bible, choosing has a clear meaning: of several possibilities, one is selected. The same word that is used to express God's interest in Israel is used when the people choose a champion to fight for them or an animal to sacrifice. God might have given the Torah to any other people, and thereby "chosen" any other people, but God did not. So the Bible authors say simply: God chose the Jews.

Here is where the problem comes in. The Bible also clearly affirms the essential equality of all human beings before God. Adam and Eve are seen as the father and mother of all humanity. We are all, then, in a very real sense, part of one family. Then what does it mean to say that the Jews, as a people, are chosen? The answer comes in the blessing we recite before the Torah is read. It praises God for "choosing us from among all peoples, by giving us the Torah." We are chosen then, to fulfill more responsibilities towards God. Most people do not think of a heavier burden of duty when they long to be singled out from everyone else. Instead, we hope to have our desires fulfilled and our joys enhanced. For us, chosenness implies greater personal satisfaction. But the Jews were chosen to serve God through a life of special duty, not to receive an abundance of privilege or power. In other words, to the extent that we were chosen, we were chosen to do more work.

Two important things to notice about this definition of chosenness. First, if following the commandments of the Torah is the way we define being chosen, then anyone is welcome to become chosen. It is not in the blood; the chosenness is not exclusive. Those who are born into the covenant are expected to fulfill it. But anyone else who is interested in following the laws of the Torah is welcome to study and learn and become a member of this chosen community. Conversion has always been a fully acceptable part of Jewish life.

Second, at the same time, conversion never has been emphasized. Jews have not gone out into the world actively looking for more people to become Jewish, so the second important element of this kind of chosenness becomes clear. To say that one is not a member of this "chosen" people does not imply anything about one's holiness or one's intimacy with God. The choice of the Jewish people to receive the Torah does not negate God's intimate relationship with the rest of humankind. Other people have different, equally valid ways of reaching God and expressing sanctity. The Jews have the Torah.

In fact, in the Book of Genesis, God makes a covenant with Noah, long before the Israelite people appear. God agrees never again to destroy humanity with a flood and Noah agrees that he and his descendants will keep the following seven commandments. All people must not: blaspheme God's name; worship idols; murder; steal; commit sexual sins; or eat a limb cut from a living animal; and all people must establish courts of justice. Seven commandments. These commandments affirm that people do not need to be Jewish to know God. The Rabbis, then, would define chosenness this way: If the rest of humanity has seven commandments to fulfill and Jews have 613 commandment to fulfill (that is, the number generally assumed in the Torah), then chosenness means undertaking to observe 606 more commandments that the rest of humanity. Why? To preserve our *particular* way of achieving a closeness with God.

The notion of chosenness is still hard for contemporary Jews to understand because we do not feel as different from the Gentiles as did the Jews of Biblical and Rabbinic times. Then Jews lived surrounded by idol worshippers. Today, Jews are clearly not the only people who believe in one God and have significant ethical concerns. As religions modernize and American life becomes more secular, we find ourselves living very much as our neighbors do. We know increasingly, unlike generations of earlier times, that humankind is truly one.

In response to this, two modern Jewish thinkers have put forth new understandings of chosenness.

Mordecai Kaplan, the founder of Reconstructionist Judaism, insisted that this principle defies reinterpretation and must be abandoned. Contrary to everything I have said, he believes that no modern person could accept a religion that has a supernatural, choosing God *and* that chosenness must imply that one group is closer to God than another. In a Reconstructionist synagogue, you would find references to chosenness removed from all prayers, including the Torah blessing.

The philosopher Martin Buber understands God by analogy to our most intimate human relationships, deep friendships or love. With regard to chosenness, Buber reminds us that all rich relationships are reciprocal, and so it is with God. Human beings have

Leaning on God

searched for God through history and occasionally had the experience that God had "been there" with them. So Buber believes that there are many true religions in human experience. But only once in human history did an ethnic group confront God and bind itself to God *as a group*, for all of history. Buber reads the Torah as the very human account of the courtship, wedding, and marriage, complete with quarrels and reconciliations, of God and the people of Israel. Other national groups had true religions. None ever transformed its ethnic life as Israel did, so that the boundary between ethnicity and religion all but disappeared. Buber suggests that just as two participants must create every genuine relationship, we may say that God, as well as the Jews, made the covenant. That is, had God not been present to the Jews in their spiritual quest, the covenant could not have come to be and endured. In this sense, for Buber, God chose, and continues to choose, the Jewish people.

Whether or not God chooses the Jewish people in any way may be a moot point, something we are simply not given enough information about in this life to completely understand, much like the question of belief in God itself. It may have been a more pressing question for our ancestors. But we who are the bearers of this particular history and tradition, we who have inherited 5,000 years of commandments and historical experience, *we* are chosen by the experiences of generation after generation of Jews. We are chosen to fulfill, as they fulfilled, the wide ranging commandments of our tradition. We are chosen to fulfill the commandments of the Torah because we know that, for our people, this particular way of life enriches us and brings us closer to God. So we *chose* to follow the commandments of the Torah – and so we become chosen.

OUR PART OF THE COVENANT

I want to say a few words to you now, before we read the Ten Commandments from the Torah, about the nature of this festival we are celebrating, *Shavuot*.

Covenant is the word of the day. It is an odd word, one that we do not use very often. Strange, then, that it is the single best word to describe what it is to be Jewish. A covenant: a binding and solemn agreement by two or more parties to do some specified thing. In some ways, it is easier to grasp in Hebrew, *brit* (or *bris*). We are most familiar with this word when it is used to name the ceremony of circumcision, traditionally used to welcome baby boys into the Jewish world. But the word *brit* does not actually have anything to do with circumcision, or baby naming, or birth. It simply means covenant, that agreement into which human beings enter when they accept the description Jew. To be Jewish is to be part of a *brit*, a covenant.

Shavuot is the time when we are to take a look at how well we are doing at fulfilling our part of this covenant. You know how the deal went: we agreed, through the voices of our ancestors who actually stood at Sinai, to fulfill the obligations of the Torah – to study words of Torah and to follow its laws, symbolized most often by the Ten Commandments. And God agreed to be there, to be present to us, to be part of our lives.

Most of the year, we are most concerned with whether or not the Godly side of the bargain is being fulfilled. As modern people, we question whether God's presence is available to us, whether, when we call out to God in need or in pain, God will be there. In our search for God, we often forget that there is a mutuality to this covenant, that we are supposed to be doing something too, especially if we are to insist that God make Godself present to us.

But what do we give? What are our commitments? Or do we, in the main, expect to receive – from God, from Judaism, from the synagogue? How often do we renege on our part of the covenant, the *brit*, through our failure to mark it on Sabbaths, for instance, or to confirm it through acts of social justice?

Yet we expect God always to be there. Sometimes when I am searching for a sense of God's presence, and am unable to experience it, I like to think that, "Oh well! *God* must have great theater tickets tonight," as I have so often heard as a reason for not being in *shul* on a particular *Shabbat*. We wish to hold God to a full-time commitment but, on examination, *our* commitment sometimes seems to be very meager indeed.

Our Part of the Covenant

It is a two-way contract, this covenant, this *brit*. It is not just something to enrich us. It is also something we are bound to. We owe something to it as well.

To imagine that we do not have any obligations to Judaism is to imagine us, as our ancestors were, after the Exodus from Egypt. Having experienced the God who led them out of bondage to freedom, they were completely free. Wandering in the wilderness, the nothingness was not satisfying. They counted forty-nine days, or seven weeks, of nothingness – no direction, no content to their religious lives, no commitment. Then, on this day of *Shavuot*, a name that in fact means "weeks," when they finally stood at the foot of Mt. Sinai, they were introduced to the specifics of their part of the covenant, the obligations of having a relationship with God.

It is such a hard concept for modern people to grasp, that we owe something to God, that being Jewish demands something of us. But there it is.

Tonight we need to ask: to what obligations does our Judaism bind us? As a symbolic answer, we read the Ten Commandments. They represent for us both the minimum obligation we sought to take on, plus our obligation to continue a serious, ongoing consideration of which other commandments, *mitzvot*, we feel bind us. The content of our commitment is debatable. It may be different for each person; we are not Orthodox Jews. But in calling ourselves Reform Jews, we do not say, "We are not bound, we have no obligations," only that we have a larger say in determining the exact nature of our obligations.

The chapter leading up to the giving of the Ten Commandments, Chapter 19 of Exodus, is meant to invoke a sense of awe and solemnity.

Listen to it carefully and, just as, at our Passover Seders, we were to experience the Exodus from Egypt as if we, ourselves, had been there, imagine that we, too, are standing at Sinai. Feel yourself there. You are there, about to receive in your hand, the Ten Commandments. It is awesome. And it requires something back. The experience asks, will you name your commitments to Judaism, will you do something to fulfill your side of the bargain?

Listen and imagine yourselves there:

> And Moses went up to God. The Lord called to him from the mountain, saying, "Thus shall you say to the house of Jacob and declare to the children of Israel: 'You have seen what I did to the Egyptians, how I bore you on eagles' wings and brought you to Me. Now then, if you will obey Me faithfully and keep My covenant, you shall be My treasured possession among all the peoples. . . .' "
>
> Moses came and summoned the elders of the people and put before them all the words that the Lord had commanded him. All the people answered as one, saying, "All that the Lord has spoken we will do!" And Moses brought back the people's words to the Lord.

And so we are there at Sinai. And we read the words most often associated with our end of the bargain, of our covenant:

> I, the Lord, am your God who brought you out of the land of Egypt, the house of bondage.
>
> You shall have no other gods beside Me.
>
> You shall not invoke the name of the Lord your God with malice.
>
> Remember the Sabbath Day and keep it holy.
>
> Honor your father and mother, that you may long endure in the land that the Lord your God gives to you.

Our Part of the Covenant

You shall not murder.

You shall not commit adultery.

You shall not steal.

You shall not bear false witness against your neighbor.

You shall not covet your neighbor's house. You shall not covet your neighbor's wife, nor his servants, nor his cattle, nor anything that is your neighbor's.

On this festival of *Shavuot*, may we renew our commitment, our *brit*.

BLESSING: A CONNECTION TO GOD

Many of you know that I moved recently. In the inevitable sorting through boxes of old papers and memorabilia, I came across a folder I had not seen in a very long time. It was pretty beat up and the edges were frayed. Written on the folder's edge were the words: Carole Meyers, *NASO*, June 6, 1970. Inside the folder, only one slip of paper remained – a yellowed but legible copy of exactly the Torah portion we read today, including the *Y'varechecha*, the priestly blessing. Twenty one years ago, I stood at a lectern not too different from this one, and read Torah for the first time, these same words read today, the words the leader of the community uses to transmit God's blessing to the people.

And look what happened to me!

Blessing: A Connection to God

While I do not remember what I said in my speech that morning, I do remember that the Rabbi spoke about Star Trek. He pointed out that the Vulcan greeting, in which the fingers of each hand were separated into a "V", and the hands held palms up with the two thumbs touching at the tips, was based on the way the priests were thought to have held their hands when they pronounced this divine blessing. You can see this symbol on the front of my lectern, designating the place of the Rabbi. Looking at it you might be able to see more easily that the fingers are being held in the shape of the Hebrew letter *Shin*, which stands for *Shaddai*, one of the names of God, meaning "Almighty." You often, by the way, see that design of the Shin on mezuzahs. Both the priests and the mezuzahs are trying to extend God's blessing over us, in a protective kind of way. But the writers of Star Trek knew Jewish tradition, and now there's a whole generation or two of people who think this sign was taken from the Vulcan greeting.

Be that as it may, the power of the blessing itself seems undiminished. The words are so simple. Here they are, translated literally:

> May God bless you and keep you.
> May God's face shine upon you and give you grace.
> May God lift up his face to you, and give you peace.

As beautiful as the words are, and especially as beautiful as the Hebrew is – it rhymes, and is alliterative, and seems to grow and spill over, in language that itself is so full – the power of the blessing comes *not* from its content, but from the very idea of being blessed, and from the history of being blessed in these particular words.

It is so unusual in our contemporary world for one person to bless another. Perhaps at the time of an engagement, young people might go to the parents and ask for a blessing. At the time of a death, especially of a parent, one might hope for a blessing. It is as if we want to take something of the person who is doing the blessing with us, to protect us and guide us.

This, exactly, is what the priestly blessing is trying to do, except that the priest, or the Rabbi, or the parents who might bless their children on *Erev Shabbat* with these words, is not so much giving of him or herself, but is trying to invoke something so much larger and more powerful and more pervasive. May all that is alive in the universe come together to bless you and guide you and protect you. May whatever powers exist, powers that we just do not understand, be on your side. It is not so much the Rabbi or the priest or the parent who is actually doing the blessing – it's as if the blessing actually disappears for a moment, and that person's body and voice are being used as a conduit for something so much more – for something we might hope to call God's presence.

And so the text says: These are the words you shall use to bless the people of Israel, but *I* shall bless them.

Now, if you are of an extremely rational mind, or, if you are starting to feel in need of an exorcist, there is a second way to understand the power of this blessing.

That is, the blessing is so old. These very words have been used to bless the birth of so many babies, the coming together of so many couples in marriage, the presence of so many Jews who have come together in prayer. In the days of the Second Temple, this blessing was recited each morning, after the morning sacrifice. It came into the traditional prayers to be said upon arising, and so the words have been spoken by hundreds of thousands of individuals, pious Jews going through their solitary morning routine. In many congregations, over the years, it has been used as the concluding benediction of services; in our congregation, it has been used on family night, to acknowledge the occasions of birthdays and anniversaries and other special moments.

So these words have been hallowed by use. They represent the combined hopes and aspirations of countless numbers of our people, our ancestors, who lifted their voices in prayer and who had faith in life. Generations who came before us, people who suffered all the travails of human life, in the main had hope and faith. They expressed them in *these* words, each time they wanted to pass them on to someone else.

Ultimately, it is a blessing to be blessed. We let go of the often silly idea that we have control over our lives, and we put ourselves, momentarily at least, in the hands of God, or in the hands of our ancestors, and lean on their words of faith for our strength.

GOD'S FOUR BLESSINGS TO US

This week's Torah portion consists of the last chapters of Leviticus. The subject matter is troubling; it deals with retribution. Many times throughout the Torah we come across the notion that those who fulfill God's commandments, those who are moral and pious, will be richly rewarded, while those who break the covenant will, in turn, be duly punished. It is an age-old issue and a frustrating one, for the simple reason that we see, on a daily basis, so many examples that seem to disprove it. We see good people who are deeply pained; we see evil people who apparently prosper. We have to wonder why; the Bible certainly suggests that this is not the way things should be.

But I have always been of the opinion that, contrary to popular belief, religion is not in the business of answering "why" questions. There are certainly numerous interpretations of these kinds of Biblical passages which attempt to reconcile the Biblical views with life as we experience it. Still, I suspect that we remain frustrated by the issue because the interpretations are just that – interpretations, not definite answers, not justifiable reasons.

I find that much of the value of religious life comes not in searching for answers to the "why" questions, but in learning to shift our perceptions. It is better that we form the questions in a less troubling way. It is better that we attempt to find meaning in what we *do* know about life, rather than frustrate ourselves with the struggle to understand things which perhaps we *cannot* know about life.

What we do know about life, from this Torah portion, is the manner in which those who follow the laws of God will be blessed. We have a specific account of those things our Torah cites as the richest of all blessings. They are only four in number. To those who keep the covenant and observe the commandments, God is first to grant a climate which will cause remarkably abundant crops. In other words, we are to be blessed with plenty to eat. Second, we are to be protected from war, so that we may go about our lives free from the fear of sudden, violent attack. Third, we are to "be fruitful and multiply." We are to see children's children; our people are to increase. Finally, God promises to bless us by allowing us to experience a divine presence. "I will be present in your midst. I will be your God and you shall be my people."

All we are promised in this passage are four really very uncomplicated and often attainable things: food, physical safety, future generations, and moments of nearness to God. We are not promised unbounded wealth. We are not promised lives free of struggle or disease. We are not even promised that each of us will be fortunate enough to raise children – only that, in the long run, our people will increase. We are not promised a complete understanding of the divine — only that we will sense God's presence in our midst.

I have to stop and wonder at the fact that, for all the difficulties and painful times in our lives, so many of us experience these four blessings so much of the time: food, safety, future generations, an awareness of God's presence. My wonderment at our fairly regular lack of appreciation and acknowledgment of these blessings reminded me of a recent New Yorker editorial I would like to share with you.

> From time to time, people complain that the papers don't print any good news. It isn't entirely true. But good news is not a newspaper's job. Psychologically, there is something reassuring about the newspaper because it is full of bad news — the same bad news each morning. . . . There is no sense reacting, we think; this is how the world is. Everything bad has already happened, and will happen again.
>
> Occasionally, when something does give us pause, likely as not it's only because it is something freakish — something we hadn't worried about before — and we accept it into our picture of the inevitable world, and read about it from then on with detachment. Last week, Kitty Wolf was driving her grandson Robert to the airport so that he could catch a flight back to school. When they were near Exit 13-A on the New Jersey turnpike, more than a hundred ounce-and-a-half jars of Dickinson's Pure Fancy Sweet Orange Marmalade fell from the sky, shattering the windshield of the car but not hurting anyone seriously. The jellies apparently fell from a transcontinental airliner, but no one knows just how. "It's a puzzlement trying to find out how it happened," an airline

spokesman told the Times. If every single morning, or even twice a month, you opened the paper to find an account of grocery items falling onto passing Volkswagens, Mrs. Wolf's travail would not be so arresting. But marmalade – marmalade, usually marvelously inert, an inmate of its jar until you choose otherwise and reach for a knife. Here it is, though, in the exit lane of the New Jersey turnpike, an orange bolt from the blue. It is hard to imagine a more meaningless story; yet, and this is truly sad, it made us think twice as hard as any food riot in Santo Domingo.*

The line from this article that stands out in my mind most clearly is this: "There is no sense reacting; this is how the world is." We seem to get to a point where not only can we no longer react to the pain in the world, but also we can no longer react to the blessings in our world. We are blinded to the pain because there is so much of it and it is only the unusual that can touch us – only marmalade coming from out of the sky. And we are blinded to the blessings promised us in the Torah because we have them so much that they no longer seem sufficient.

We are aware only of the unusual, the extraordinarily good things that happen to us, which we come to think of as our right, and so we feel deprived when they do not happen. Sometimes we see instead the extraordinarily good things that happen to others, and this sight leaves us jealous and angry. Certainly we are aware of the extraordinarily bad things that happen to us, leaving us feeling cheated and demanding to know why, to know how God could have allowed such things to happen.

---
* William McKibben, Comment *The New Yorker*, May 7, 1984 P. 42.

Leaning on God

 Yet we forget to notice that, much of the time, most of us are blessed with all that God promised us: with ample food, with safety from attack, with the promise of future generations and with an occasional glimpse of the divine in our presence. It is bad enough when we see only the marmalade coming down from the sky, and can no longer respond to the life-threatening problems of our world. But it is worse when we see only the extraordinary moments of our lives, be they good or bad, and can no longer respond to the routine of goodness and prosperity against which we live our lives.

 May our eyes be opened to the blessings that surround us. On this Shabbat, may we remember that, by acknowledging these blessings and by being conscious of them, we create just a little bit more of a sense of Godliness in our troubled world.

HOLINESS

If I had to pick only one word in the entire Hebrew language to know, it would be the word which names this week's Torah portion, *Kedoshim*. *Kedoshim* means "holiness" but, like holiness itself, the word has many forms and manifestations; it overflows from one context to another, as holiness itself can flow between one person and another. The three root letters, *koff, daled, shin,* together making *Kadosh*, are found in many common Hebrew words. If we examine some of the words, it will be easier for us to see just what our tradition means when it uses this slippery word "holiness."

Every Shabbat, on most holidays, at baby-namings and at weddings – on every occasion of celebration – as Jews, we have a particular way of expressing our joy. We raise a full cup of wine to symbolize our gladness, and we say a blessing to consecrate that moment, forcing ourselves to both acknowledge and emphasize the joy we are experiencing. We say *Baruch atah adonai, eloheynu melech ha-olam, borei pri hagafen*: Praised are you, our God, ruler of the universe, creator of the fruit of the vine. We call that blessing the *kiddush*, the words through which we acknowledge our joy, *kiddesh*. Joyfulness is a part of holiness. For Jews, holiness cannot exist without joy.

A Jewish wedding ceremony is different from a civil wedding ceremony, because of the letters *koff, daled, shin*. When pronounced *kiddushin*, they refer to the bond that is contracted on the wedding day. *Kiddushin* means marriage, the entering into a particular state of holiness. What is it that is holy about becoming married? This use of the word emphasizes its meaning of separation. When two people marry, there is an emphasis on their being set apart, singled out, one for the other. A bond is created between them that separates them from all others and makes them holy. At the same time, a bond is created between these two people and God; a commitment is made to building a Jewish home and raising Jewish children. *Koff, daled, shin, mem soffis*. Marriage, separateness, is a part of holiness. For the Jew, holiness cannot exist without a sense of separateness, of setting apart.

We know *koff, daled, shin* from another common word. Pronounced *Kaddish*, these letters unlock another world of associations for us. It is with this one particular prayer, the *Kaddish*, that we remember our past – our ancestors from long ago, Abraham and Sarah, Isaac and Rebekah, Jacob, Leah and Rachel – and our own pasts, grandparents and parents who came before us and shared their lives with us. When we say the *Kaddish* we are moved by the memories of those we love who have died, and we honor them by praising God. To say the *Kaddish* is both to remember and to praise. For the Jew, holiness cannot exist without love and honor.

Holiness

The prophet Isaiah had a vision of holiness which is preserved for us in both our Bible and our prayer book. Isaiah was privileged to behold the very presence of God surrounded by angels who are chanting the words *kadosh, kadosh, kadosh, Adonai, st'vaot* - Holy, Holy, Holy, is the Lord of Hosts; the earth is filled with God's glory. Each Shabbat morning, when we stand to say the *Kedushah* prayer, we repeat these words Isaiah spoke, in awe of God's majesty and glory. For Jews, holiness cannot exist without a feeling of majesty, without awe.

Joy, separateness, love, honor, awe – we begin to see that *Kadosh* does not translate so easily, that there are many facets to holiness and many ways of experiencing holiness in our lives. It has been said that holiness is a force which can pass from one object to another. To be holy is to be the conductor for this flow of energy and to affect the world through your actions. So the word appears in the blessing we speak before fulfilling a *mitzvah*, a commandment: *baruch atah adonai elohenu melech haolam asher* kedushanu b'mitzvah tov. . . Praised are you, our God, ruler of the universe, who has sanctified us, and made us *holy* through your commandments. It is by doing your commandments, specific acts of goodness, by which we become holy.

So this Torah portion called *Kedoshim*, holiness, is not about awe and majesty, but is about specific kinds of behavior we know we must exhibit, in order to be holy: Honor mother and father, keep the Sabbath, give to the poor, do not swear falsely, treat all human beings with dignity, render your decisions in a court of law fairly and justly. For Jews, holiness cannot exist without being expressed in countless, small acts of concrete goodness.

Koff, daled, shin – holiness – to be awesome and to be concrete; to be connected by rare energy, and to be separate; to be joyful and to mourn. *Koff, daled, shin* – holiness –a concept that is so all-encompassing it can include a list of opposites, contradictory forces inside one image. To understand holiness is to understand that a thing can be one way and exactly another way, given different circumstances and definitions. To be Jewish is to understand that there exists the possibility of holiness in every action, in every moment, in every encounter. To be holy is to greet the world from the perspective of *Kedushah*, to look for the possibility of holiness in every touch, in every act, in every word.

To be human is to be one way at one time and exactly another way at a different time, depending on the circumstances and definitions. To be human is to defy perfection, to be good and loving and wise at moments, and to berate ourselves for being mean-hearted and unforgiving and stupid at others.

If to be holy can include both a thing and its opposite, then perhaps to be Jewish, that is, to make the pursuit of holiness a regular part of your life, is to accept that we cannot be perfect, that we cannot always be righteous and wise, and that even our imperfections can be part of our struggle to be good.

The most famous passage in this Torah portion is: "Love your neighbor as yourself." One Rabbi asks: "Why doesn't it simply say love your neighbor? Why add 'as yourself'? Because if a person hates himself, he cannot love his neighbor." We were each created by God with our faults and inadequacies, but nevertheless we were created by God. So somehow we must see that each of us comprises a world in which both a thing and its opposite exist. We are short-tempered, mean, and loveable. We are lazy, weak, and acceptable. Our imperfections are part of our God-given human nature – and we are commanded to love ourselves – both sides of ourselves.

Holiness

Love your neighbor as yourself means to love yourself in spite of all the imperfections. Be holy. Understand that holiness can exist in every act, in a thing and its opposite, in our good sides and our bad sides. Be holy. Assume the attitude that encourages you to make holiness out of whatever the world offers you. For while holiness can exist in anything, in a thing and its opposite, it exists only when we, finding holiness in ourselves, look for holiness in the world, and nurture it.

SMALL STEPS

Last night I sat with 25 women from the Angeles Crest Chapter of ORT. We talked and schmoozed and had a discussion about raising Jewish children, which turned into a discussion of the need to develop and articulate carefully our Jewish identities as adults. There were moments of disagreement, moments of shared understanding, fleeting tensions as one position or another was threatened. And there was a growing understanding that we are all struggling towards the same goal: a richer experience of our religious lives as Jews.

I have always found there to be an enormous amount of dignity in ORT, an organization which evolved from a nineteenth century fund designed to lift Russian Jews out of poverty (and whose initials come from Russian words encapsulating this mission.) The women meet, set fundraising goals, and go about the business of meeting those goals with a minimum of fuss and bother. Fundraising is the crux of the organization . . . or is it? One woman described all the important education and training that is made possible through the efforts of groups like this all around the country. But I came away from the meeting last night with the unmistakable feeling that these monthly meetings, this commitment to sitting and talking and sharing ideas and learning more about Jewish life, is the really important thing about Women's American ORT. These are busy women. They are mothers, working hard at creating homes and raising children and interacting with the school system to ensure quality education for the next generation, not to mention *some* separation between religion and the public school system. They are doctors, lawyers, therapists, students – active, vital women who have many important areas in their lives competing for attention. But, there they were, gathered together on a Thursday night, to talk, think, explore and grow.

There is a sense of sanctity about the entire enterprise. These are the moments in our lives we choose to devote to matters that ultimately count. What do we stand for; what do we want to pass on to our children: what really matters in our lives? They are not questions that can be answered in a single women's meeting, nor in a year of meetings. But the conviction to try was present, and it was holy.

God says to Moses, in this week's Torah portion of *Terumah*: "This is how you are to build the ark, which will house the tablets of my commandments." God then proceeds to describe, in painstaking detail, how Moses is to build each of the other objects in the Tabernacle, in the order of their holiness, the holiest objects coming first, the next holiest second, and so on. Moses, though, when he begins to build the Tabernacle, does so in the exact opposite order. He starts with the least holy object and works up, only at the end building the ark to hold the Ten Commandments. Why does Moses choose to conduct this whole enterprise of building the Tabernacle in exactly the opposite order of the way God described it, so that he is working from the least holy to the most holy objects?

The Rabbis teach: God can start with the ideal, but human beings have to work up to it. God could visualize the entire finished project. Moses, the human being, had to start where he was, barely able to visualize the first, least holy object, and able only to begin work on it. It must have been a slow and painstaking process for Moses to grasp what God wanted, and then to translate it into reality. The miracle of Moses is that he started. He started with what he *could* see, and what he was reasonably able to create within the confines of his reality. He ended up building the Tabernacle.

All of these women last night were doing what we all do – grappling with what our lives should be and in particular, with what our lives should be, Jewishly. Together, perhaps we glimpsed the ideal, but it seemed very far away. The question to be asked now is not "Will I ever reach that ideal?" Rather, the question is "Can I start where I am, and add some holiness to my life? Can I, like Moses, start with the smallest step, the least holy object; can I take that *first* step to change my patterns and habits and add a degree of holiness to my life?" A completely understood and articulated Jewish identity, translated into actions and behaviors that will encourage our children to become identified Jews is an ideal – but can I light *Shabbat* candles, or make a commitment to attending public prayer, or read a book on Jewish thought, or say the *Shema* each night with my child? Can I begin to grasp the holy, the ideal, in my relationship to Judaism, or in my relationship with my spouse, or in my vision of my own life? We do not have to live our ideals; the challenge is only to start, to entertain the ideal of the holy, to not let the holy be a foreign thing in our lives.

Small Steps

The words of the Israeli national anthem offer hope for achieving the ideal. The last lines of *Hatikvah* – The Hope – teach us:

L'hiyot am chofsi	to be a free people
B'artzenu	in our land
Eretz Tzion	in the land of Zion
B'yerushalayim	in Jerusalem

ORT does so much for the land of Israel. Sometimes, we may not see the ideal there, as the people of Israel struggle, and sometimes the actions of the Israeli Government surprise and even dismay us. So the tabernacle is not yet built. But in maintaining the hope, in taking small steps, we keep the ideal alive. It is a lesson that ORT has taught us well.

LETTING GO

More than in any other year, we have a need this year to gather in our sanctuary, to see it confirmed in each other's eyes that the Jewish community is strong and safe and willing to move forward. We will long remember that image from the attack on the North Valley Jewish Community Center – Jewish children, hand in hand, being escorted to safety. *So close* to us, Jewish children wounded, almost killed, just because they are Jewish.

We greet this New Year 5760 in a synagogue building properly prepared with security. We are reminded to be prudent in all matters of safety, just as we must continually remind ourselves of safety procedures in driving our cars, or in earthquake preparations. But I see that we are not crippled by this unspeakable attack, that we are, in fact, strengthened in our resolve to live as Jews.

Our tradition has given us a gift this year, a sign, some might say. Add up the individual numbers in the number of this New Year,

Letting Go

5760, 5+7+6+0 and what do we get but 18, the Hebrew number signifying life, *chai*. This year, of all years, we choose life, for ourselves, for our synagogue, for Jewish communities around the world. We choose life.

Now, since we have made this commitment, these High Holy Days speak their message to us ever more fiercely. What are we doing with this life? Rabbi Elazar ben Azariah said: "From all the sins before the Lord, you shall be cleansed." But how? This is my observation: Year after year, we engage in this process of repentance. Even so, there is a weight that remains with us at the end of *Yom Kippur* day, a burden that does not lift, though we do the work and say the prayers.

What we rarely address is the feelings we are left with when we are sinned against and when we sin. Having been sinned against, we know what it is to feel shamed and humiliated. We have felt embarrassed and afraid. We have felt stupid, belittled, diminished and demeaned. The childhood versions of these experiences are easier to name than the adult ones. You know them: not being picked for a team, being laughed at for giving the wrong answer, not being told the secret that everyone else knows. As adults, we carry the emotional residue of these cruelties, and, although we have better defenses, we can still feel battered by sins committed against us. We may have been cheated, or lied to, misled, or left out, wronged in any way, and although it is we who have been wronged, we may still have feelings of shame or humiliation.

And what does it feel like to have shamed another, to have humiliated someone, embarrassed him or her? What does it feel like to have made someone afraid? Ask yourself, what have you done to demean, to diminish your friends, your children, your spouse, your parents, your employees? When have you yelled, instead of explained, criticized instead of taught, accused instead of trusted, lost your temper, instead of coped?

Others wound us; we wound others.

We may forgive the wounder, but how do we rid ourselves of the feelings the wound has engendered? When do we say "I have been humiliated and now I have moved through it, and beyond it. I need not spend the rest of my days feeling humiliated." We may forgive the one who has embarrassed us, but when do we stop feeling like an embarrassed person, so defensive, out of our fear that we will be embarrassed again and again.

In the midst of all this mess, *Vayikra*, God calls out to us. *Vayikra* is the Hebrew name of the third book of the Torah, Leviticus, the one that seems least relevant to our lives. But this year I hear God calling out to us from the pages of that much-maligned text. Leviticus contains something that seems to me so precious this year. The ancient Israelites absolutely understood the concepts of pure and impure, clean and unclean – in Hebrew, *tahor* and *tamey*. They knew this had nothing to do with physical cleanliness, but everything to do with powerful forces in nature that could affect one's sense of wholeness. For them, one was in a state of purity until rendered unclean by contact with things like a dead body, or childbirth, or sins of any kind. Carefully elaborated in Leviticus 16 is the process by which one could move from a state of uncleanness to cleanness. It is, of course, the system of sacrifices, ancient and eerie and gory, and at the same time dramatic and effective.

Listen to the ancient *Yom Kippur* ritual. The high priest Aaron prepares by bathing and putting on the simplest robe of white linen. He enters the Holy of Holies. He brings with him a bull and a goat. Aaron slaughters the bull as a sin offering before God, and he repeats the

Letting Go

formulaic words asking for forgiveness. Aaron then places two handfuls of finely ground incense in his fire pan, and burns them, filling the Holy of Holies with an aromatic cloud of smoke. Mysteriously, he sprinkles the blood of the bull with his finger first over the east side of the covering of the ark, then seven times over the front of the cover.

There is another step in the drama. A goat is brought before Aaron. He lays both his hands upon its head and confesses over it all the sins of the Israelites. That goat is sent out into the wilderness, carrying away all their iniquities. (This, of course, is the origin of the concept of a scapegoat.) Aaron then removes the ritual clothing, bathes in water once again, and dresses in clean clothes.

And it is done. He has stepped from one realm into another, left the unclean for the clean, and is prepared to present himself, pure, before God.

Vayikra, God is calling out to us, from the mysterious realm of sacrificial offerings and the sending of goats into the wilderness. God knows what it is for human beings to feel impure and defiled, and is teaching us that we must find the courage to put an end to it, to use a ritual that will move us, from the realm of the unclean into the realm of the clean.

Rabbi Yitzchak of Vorki notes that the confession of sins we recite on *Yom Kippur* is done in alphabetical order – *ashamnu, bagadnu, gazalnu* – and wonders why. He answers: there is no end to our sins, but there must be an end to repentance. When you have come to the end of the alphabet, you are done.

What we require is a ritual that will let us be done with all the old feelings that are the product of our having sinned, and having been sinned against. We need a moment, an action, a drama to be played out, that will give us release and lift the burden.

I am not recommending animal sacrifice.

But if we were creative and brave, we could design, each for ourselves, a ritual that would have the power to move us from the unclean to the clean. The ritual would include naming the feelings of uncleanness we bear, and recalling the experiences that caused them. And there would be an action taken, after which you could say: "I'm done with that. It's over."

We each have a different level of attraction to ritual. Some of these suggestions may make you wince, but you can create the ritual that will work for you.

Imagine, for example, writing the experiences you wish to be released from on paper . . . and burning that paper, as if it were Aaron's aromatic incense.

Imagine immersing yourself in water, as Aaron did before he entered the Holy of Holies. It does not matter where – in the ocean, in your own pool, in a *mikva*, in a public swimming pool. What matters is that you would hold in your mind all the feelings, all the uncleanness, and let go of it, as you felt the waters swirl around you.

Imagine adapting *tashlich*, the traditional ritual in which crumbs that have accumulated in your pockets become the symbol for sins that have accumulated in your life. On *Rosh Hashanah* afternoon you cast the sins away, as you cast the crumbs into a lake or a stream. Imagine instead, that what is cast away are the feelings of uncleanness. Say: "I am done with these feelings. They no longer define me, or determine the way I will act in the world."

I believe that doing *tzedakah* can make a powerful ritual moment. Perhaps you articulate the uncleanness, and you make a pact with yourself; "when I serve food at the homeless shelter in January," you say, "it will be my offering. When I complete that act of *tzedakah*, I will free myself of these feelings." Or, choose a charity to give money to, one that strives to make the world the way you believe it should be, and write a check, as generously as you can. Resolve that when you mail that check, you will be released from your uncleanness. When it flows into the sea of envelopes, disappearing from sight, you move from the state of impurity to the state of purity.

There are some who have no tolerance for ritual at all, especially modern ritual. Still, you can choose a moment, a silent moment, with no action attached to it, but a moment of private awareness and resolve. "I am calling a truce, an end to that pain. I am at the end of the alphabet, and not only are my sins repented for, but I am done with these crippling feelings. I am moving now, from the unclean to the clean."

Vayikra, God is calling out to us; I know you may not hear Him. Are you surprised that I say Him? Perhaps it is Her? Or It? Today it does not matter. Just believe, for today, because I am asking you to, that there is an eternal soul to the universe, a soul indescribably beyond even the magnificence of our souls, yours and mine. It is only waiting for you to find your way back to cleanse you, to make you clean. It, God, She, He – has the power to move you beyond where you are.

Just lean on it. We so much want to lean on something, someone, for help. Go on, you can, it is there. *Vayikra* – God is calling out to us.

The more usual tasks of the season still must be done. This ritual purification cannot take the place of repentance, of making amends for the wrong things we have done, of asking and granting forgiveness. But if we have participated in a ritual restoring of our purity, I believe the experience of the end of *Yom Kippur* day can be something quite remarkable.

Leaning on God

We will have been in services all day. We will have opened our hearts to the chanting of the *Kol Nidre*. We will have fasted and prayed. Imagine us now concluding, standing in front of the open ark for ever so long, until we think we might faint. Finally we cry "*Adonai hu ha-Elohim*" – The Eternal is God – seven times. We hear the final blast of the *shofar* and, at that moment, it will be possible to feel a great sense of forgiveness, release, and peace. Not only have our sins been forgiven, but our purity has been restored. We can enter the New Year weightless, open, loving.

This is what I wish for you this New Year of life, 5760. In the words of the last verse of *Adon Olam*:

> With my whole body and soul
> I place myself in God's hand
> When I sleep and when I wake.
> God is with me; I will not fear.

THE POWER TO MOVE FORWARD

The exodus from Egypt, the legend of our struggle from slavery to freedom is a wonder, but it is also troublesome. This is the story that contains one of the great miracles of the Bible. The people were suffering under the harsh rule of the Pharaoh and they cried out to God, and God heard them. God sent Moses to free the people from the hands of the oppressor. Moses reasoned, then pleaded, then argued with Pharaoh; he threatened and then he brought the plagues. He convinced Pharaoh, finally, to let the Israelite people go.

But the volatile Pharaoh changed his mind, sending troops of soldiers in pursuit of the Israelite people. And the people were trapped. In front of them they faced the solid depths of the Red Sea; behind them they faced the oncoming blood-thirsty soldiers of Pharaoh. Trapped. With nowhere to go, the people once again turned to God.

Leaning on God

Our tradition tells us that God gave Moses the power to split the Red Sea in half, so that the waters separated into two great walls, leaving a path of dry ground for the people to cross over onto land. When the people of Israel had crossed through the Red Sea, the Sea returned to its normal state, destroying Pharaoh's army as it did so.

Az Yashir Moshe u'venai Yisrael. Then Moses and the Israelites sang this song to the Lord. "I will sing to the Lord for he has triumphed gloriously. Horse and driver he has hurled into the sea. The Lord is my strength and might, he is become my salvation."

No matter how much we enjoy the story, no matter how much pleasure we take in the Passover ritual, the events bother us. Miracles are not for us. The fact that the people were miraculously saved in this way somehow makes us take the story less seriously than we otherwise might.

But miracles worked for the Biblical authors. For them, the fact that it was possible for God to intervene in the world of natural events and change reality was comforting. The working of miracles underscored God's power for them. The Biblical authors simply do not question God's ability to do anything by any means. As a result, the occurrence of the physical miracle itself, the splitting of the Red Sea, did not become the main point of the story for them.

Not being troubled by whether such a thing could occur, the Biblical mind was able to understand clearly where the emphasis in the story belonged. The people of Israel were brought out of the land of Egypt and taught to treasure freedom. Since they had experienced oppression at the hands of the Egyptians, it became fundamental to their world view not to oppress others.

Some thousand years later the writers of the Talmud already had much more in common with us today. They were troubled by the

The Power to Move Forward

notion that a supernatural power could step into history and alter the natural course of events. One Talmudic writer argues that the splitting of the Red Sea was preordained and accounted for in the act of creation. Rabbi Yochanon actually said that God made a condition with the sea, at the time of its creation, that it would part before the children of Israel. Another Talmudic author pictures Moses arguing with God. Can you imagine it, Moses himself saying: "But God, it would involve a breach of your own act of creation." The Talmudist pictures God responding calmly and wisely, "But Moses, you have not read the beginning of the Torah; I made the splitting of the Red Sea a condition of the world at the time of creation."

Some years later, a story was written by a Rabbi who viewed the occurrence altogether differently. This version is rooted in the *midrash* about Nachshon being the courageous one to step first into the Red Sea. He said: "The people of Israel were indeed trapped. They faced the depths of the Red Sea before them and the hordes of Pharaoh's army behind them." He acknowledges that the people cried out to God for help but then this author says something different. He says, "The people of Israel began to walk into the water. They were not frozen by their fear; they were not willing to concede defeat. With no possibility of turning back and nowhere to go forward, they *went forward anyway*. They found the courage to take those first steps right into the depths of the Red Sea, because they knew there was nothing to do but go forward. The people walked into the water up to their ankles, up to their knees, up to their waists, and still they continued, with the faith that somehow it would come out all right. They knew they had no choice but to move forward, up to their shoulders, up to their chins." The story goes that the people of Israel walked into the waters of the Red Sea until the water reached their nostrils when,

Leaning on God

suddenly, the waters split, and they were able to continue forward on dry land. Miracles do happen, this Rabbi concludes, when we give them a chance to happen.

Our rational brains still kick into action. We know that this story does not solve our fundamental problem — how could it be that a great body of water split into two parts? And yet, something in me is satisfied by this sacred legend. It puts one back in the same position as the biblical author, because it takes the emphasis off the physical miracle itself and puts it somewhere else in the story. Biblical people were not obsessed with the miracle; they were obsessed with the concept of freedom.

As moderns, we cannot allow ourselves to be obsessed with our scientific questioning of the events of the Bible. We must ask what meaning we *can* find in them. Hundreds and hundreds of years ago, one Rabbi suggested that we can make miracles happen if we are courageous enough to initiate them, if only by simply keeping on going. In our world, that is sometimes the hardest thing to do.

So many times in our lives, we replay the scenario of the Israelite people caught between two dead-ends, feeling as if we cannot move forward, yet knowing that there is nowhere to return.

I recently saw an interview with a famous actress on television. The interviewer was reckless enough to ask her if, with all her stardom, she didn't get lonely sometimes. She stared at him blankly for a moment and then said "that she believed that everyone was scared and lonely all the time, that being scared and lonely are a constant in life, and that you had to just ignore it, and go ahead anyway." And I thought to myself: "going ahead anyway" is a miracle. And I pictured in my mind the Israelite people up to their nostrils in the Red Sea.

The Power to Move Forward

Often, when I tell the Nachshon story, and talk about the Israelites not being able to go forward or backward, I see a flicker of recognition in our kids' eyes, even at very young ages. They are enthralled with the story; they recognize the confused, mixed-up feeling of being stuck with no clear-cut solution in sight. I often think that if this story teaches them that they must find the courage within themselves to go forward anyway, it is indeed a miracle.

This particular Sabbath, on which we read the story of the Exodus, has a special name. It is not called the Sabbath of the miracle, but it is called *Shabbat Shira*, the Sabbath of the Song. The emphasis is not on the fact that a miracle happened or on how it happened. The emphasis instead is on the joy and the exuberance the Israelites felt after they forced themselves to go forward.

Perhaps the strong east wind really did blow hard enough to split the Red Sea – and perhaps it didn't. Perhaps God actually intervened in human history and suspended the laws of nature – and perhaps that cannot be.

The important thing is that the Israelite people went forward, when it looked like there was nowhere to go. The Israelite people went forward and they found freedom, and that is a miracle.

Az Yashir Moshe u'venai Yisrael. Then Moses and all Israel sang:

Mi Chamocha Bo'alim Adonai. "Who is like you, O God, who gives us the strength to go forward and to create miracles."

EPILOGUE

LEANING ON GOD, PART III: EULOGY ON THE DEATH OF RABBI CAROLE MEYERS*

What does a person do when she learns she has cancer? Carole first learned the diagnosis on May 17, 2007. We thought she had strained her back playing handball with our kids, or at most had a herniated disk. Possibly some sort of dreaded surgery would be needed to repair the disk. But cancer? It didn't seem possible. Yet there it was.

I do not know how I myself would react if it had been I, rather than she. But her response was extraordinary. Her mind, her very

---

* By Ralph Zarefsky. Delivered at Rabbi Meyers' funeral on July 31, 2007, by Reverend Philip B. Wood.

instinct, did not take her to depression or to feeling sorry for herself; it went instead to Biblical text, to the story of Jacob sleeping in the desert, and dreaming of the ladder with angels ascending and descending. "Surely," Jacob says to himself, "God is in this place and I, I did not know it." Like other rabbis, Carole was taken with the repetition of the word I: *I*, I did not know it. And what she drew from this experience was the discovery – despite the insidiousness of the disease – of the presence of the holy.

She wrote:

> God was in this place and I, who had never as yet had so much fear in me, and so much taken away from me, I was still able to sense God's Presence in lived life. To thank God. The sense of uplift was magnificent. I did not feel abandoned, or alone. I did not feel angry. I did feel God suffering beside me, silently wishing and hoping and thinking that this was not the way matters should stand . . . .

Carole felt buoyed, protected, uplifted, by the collective strength of the communities in which we live, through the numbers of people who brought us daily dinners, who picked up our kids from school and took them to appointments or ball games, who went shopping for us, who sent flowers and cards and e-mails and telephone messages. She wrote:

> Their joy in doing an act of goodness, an act of true *tzedakah* in helping us walk through one difficult moment to another, is so moving to me. And the simple idea that they are doing good through the work of their hands in preparing us a meal is sustaining us on so many different levels that it is not simple at all, but as profound as can be.

Eulogy on the Death of Rabbi Carole Meyers

This was Carole at her essence. To see the holy in the world around us, whether in the severe test of a life-ending disease, or, more usually, in the mundane activities of everyday life. She reveled in the folk wisdom of her favorite artist, country-western singer Jerry Jeff Walker: "Life's too short to brush and floss." She took an idea and teased out its spiritual nugget and people saw the holy that she had uncovered. She inspired people, and taught by her inspiration.

She had a passion for life, a radiance that spread illumination, a brilliance cocooned in a gentle soothing voice. She preached with insight, but without bombast, and she counted it a success, not a failure, when the community joined her in prayer and song, rather than being passive and letting someone preach or sing at them. She had an uncanny ability to empathize, and to connect with other people by listening to their personal stories. As she lay dying, I saw her in the doctor's office receiving what turned out to be the one dose of chemotherapy she could tolerate, and as she did so it was she who was listening and the nurse who was telling her story, with Carole nodding and giving advice.

And for all these things she was to others, she saved the best for her family, for me and our two boys. She turned down an offer from a prominent temple in the East so that we could be married and make our lives here. She turned aside the entreaties of the seminary in New York to help administer that institution so that we could have our second child in this community. She gave up a congregation that adored her in order to replenish herself and to attend to the really important part of life: helping with homework, going to youth basketball games, arranging play dates, and imbuing our boys with the right core values. She would say to them as they left the house: remember who you are and where you came from.

Leaning on God

On our wedding day, we walked down the aisle to the sweet Hebrew song of *Dodi Li*. The words mean "My Beloved is Mine." The song is melodic in Hebrew, and touching in its meaning:

> Who is this, rising up from the desert
> Who is she, rising up?
> Perfumed with myrrh and frankincense
> Myrrh and frankincense.

And then, shortly thereafter, we know:

> You have captured my heart, my bride.

One of the last times before Carole became so ill that she could not walk, but at a time when she could still shuffle with my facing her, holding her hands and walking backwards, we moved down the hall to the stairs leading up to our bedroom, my point to her counterpoint. Softly we sang *Dodi Li*, from beginning to end, beginning – and ending – with *dodi li*: My beloved is mine and I am hers.

Carole captured my heart. She was my lover, my companion, my best friend, the mother of our children. *Shalom*, my sweet. You kept God. May God now keep you.

www.ingramcontent.com/pod-product-compliance
Lightning Source LLC
Chambersburg PA
CBHW070528090426
42735CB00013B/2908